SWIFT BOAT DOWN

to: Bob Howell,

   Another lost RV Travel we
met in Gallup, NM with broken
RV's, Good luck with your trip,
much short than mine, enjoy
the rest of it,
   Warm Regards from a fellow California
[signature] "anther' Swift Boat Down"
             June 2006

SWIFT BOAT DOWN

The Real Story of the Sinking of PCF-19

James Steffes ENC
Retired

Library of Congress Number:		2005907931
ISBN:	Hardcover	1-59926-613-X
	Softcover	1-59926-612-1

This book was printed in the United States of America.

To order additional copies of this book, contact:
Xlibris Corporation
1-888-795-4274
www.Xlibris.com
Orders@Xlibris.com
29786

Contents

FORWARD

T HIS BOOK IS DEDICATED TO THE CREW OF PCF-19, SUNK OFF THE COAST OF NORTH VIETNAM ON 16 JUNE 1968. FOUR MEN WERE KILLED THAT NIGHT UNDER VERY UNUSUAL CIRCUMSTANCES. ONLY NOW CAN THEIR STORY BE TOLD. WHAT FOLLOWS IS THE A TRUE ACCOUNT OF WHAT REALLY HAPPENED AS RECALLED BY THE SURVIVORS OF PCF-19, PCF-12, USCG POINT DUME, U.S. MARINES ASHORE AND MEN STATIONED ABOARD U.S. NAVY SHIPS OPERATING IN THE AREA. THE FACTS NOW REVEALED IN THE OFFICIAL DECK LOGS AND THE MEMORIES OF THE MEN WHO WERE THERE DIFFER FROM THE NEWS MEDIA COVERAGE OF THE STORY. SUNK BY FRIENDLY FIRE WAS THE NEWSPAPER STORY, A STORY THAT REVEALS A RELUCTANCE TO ACCUSE AN ENEMY OF ESCALATION DURING A TIME WHEN THE PARIS PEACE TALKS WERE BEING ORGANIZED. THIS WAS A GREAT DISERVICE TO THESE BRAVE MEN ABOARD PCF-19 AND A TERRIBLE BURDEN FOR THE F-4 PHANTOM PILOT WHO WAS BLAMED FOR THE INCIDENT IN THE PRESS.

THE STORY WILL BE TOLD IN THREE PARTS. FIRST, I WILL GIVE SOME BACKGROUND INTO THE MISSION AND THE CONDITIONS IN THE AREA LEADING UP TO THE INCIDENT. SECOND, THE INCIDENT AS IT ACTUALLY HAPPENED AS RELATED BY WITNESSES ABOARD SHIPS AND THE OFFICIAL ACCOUNT OF THAT NIGHT. THIRD, THE FOLLOWUP INVESTIGATION BY OTHERS AND MYSELF TO REACH THE CONCLUSION OF HOSTILE FIRE CAUSING THE SINKING OF PCF-19 WAS BASED ON OFFICIAL LOGS AND RECORDS AND EYE WITNESS ACCOUNTS. A SUMMARY OF THE DETAILS BACKED BY DOCUMENTED PROOF OF HOSTILE FIRE WILL DETAIL THE REAL STORY BEHIND THE SINKING OF PCF-19. NOTHING CAN CHANGE THE "OFFICIAL FINDINGS" OF THE COMMAND AUTHORITY AT THE TIME BUT THE TRUTH AS I OBSERVED IT FROM THE DECK OF PCF-12 WOULD NOW BE TOLD.

A SPECIAL TRIBUTE

I n addition to the crew of PCF-19, this book is dedicated to all of the Swift Boat Sailors who lost their lives serving aboard these small but mighty gunboats. Here are their names;

PATROL CRAFT FAST DIVISION—101 (An Thoi)

2/14/66   BM1 Tommy E. Hill, Knoxville, TN—(Gulf of Thailand) PCF-4 Remote Mine Explosion Baie De Cau Dong River South of Rach Gia near Three Sisters Mountain Area (Kien Giang Province)

2/14/66   EN2 Jack C. Rodriguez, Jackson Heights, NY—(Gulf of Thailand) PCF-4 Remote Mine Explosion Baie De Cau Dong River South of Rach Gia Near Three Sisters Mountain Area (Kien Giang Province)

2/14/66   GMG2 Dayton L. Rudisill, Greensburg, KS—(Gulf of Thailand) PCF-4 Remote Mine Explosion Baie De Cau Dong River South of Rach Gia Near Three Sisters Mountain Area (Kien Giang Province)

2/14/66   SN David J. Boyle, Woodland, CA—(Gulf of Thailand) PCF-4 Remote Mine Explosion Baie De Cau Dong River South of Rach Gia Near Three Sisters Mountain Area (Kien Giang Province)

10/18/66   BM2 Hubert Tuck Jr., Lenoir City, TN—(Gulf of Thailand) PCF-9 81mm Mortar Explosion Conducting Shore Bombardment (Kien Giang Province)

10/18/66   EN2 Gale J. Hays, Falling Rock, WV—(Gulf of Thailand) PCF-9 81mm Mortar Explosion Conducting Shore Bombardment (Kien Giang Province)

10/18/66   QM3 Eugene L. Self, Carteret, NJ—(Gulf of Thailand) PCF-9 81mm Mortar Explosion Conducting Shore Bombardment (Kien Giang Province)

COASTAL DIVISION ELEVEN (An Thoi)

9/4/68   RD3 Gerald D. Pochel, Otis, OR—(An Xugen Province) PCF-96 Cua Long River Ca Mau Peninsula

11/3/68   BM3 Richard C. Simon, Ellsworth, WI—(An Xugen Province) PCF-50 Song Ong Doc River Ca Mau Peninsula (Operation Seafloat)

12/6/68   BM2 Steve R. Luke, Provo, UT—(An Xugen Province) PCF-36 Bo De River Cau Mau Peninsula (Operation Seafloat)

1/5/69   BM3 Gerald R. Horrell, North Hollywood, CA—(An Xugen Province) PCF-71 Song Ong Doc River(Operation Seafloat)

4/12/69   LT Donald G. Droz, Rich Hill, MO—1100 (An Xugen Province) PCF-43 OinC Rach Duong Keo Canal (Operation Seafloat)

4/12/69   QM3 Thomas E. Holloway, New Castle, IN—(An Xugen Province) PCF-51 Helmsman Rach Duong Keo Canal (Operation Seafloat)

5/5/69   BM3 Richard L. Baumberger Jr., Mansfield, OH—(An Xugen Province) PCF-9 Rach Duong Keo Canal (Operation Seafloat)

5/15/69   EN3 Dewey R. Decker, Ionia, MI—(An Xugen Province) PCF-51 Song Bay Hap River Cau Mau Peninsula (Operation Seafloat)

5/15/69   GMG3 Richard W. Stindl, Beloit, WI—(An Xugen Province) PCF-51 Song Bay Hap River Cau Mau Peninsula (Operation Seafloat)

8/12/69   GMG3 Stephen J. Penta, Revere, MA—(An Xugen Province) PCF-57 Rach Cai Chon Nho Canan Cau Mau Peninsula (Operation Seafloat)

10/2/69   QM2 Richard L. Wissler Jr., Willow Street, PA—(An Xugen Province) PCF-27 Claymore Mine Song Ong Doc River Cau Mau Peninsula 2 ½ Miles South of ATSB Song Ong Doc (Operation Seafloat)

12/4/69   RD3 Martin S. Doherty, New York, NY—(An Xugen Province) PCF-50 Peak Tank Gunner Dam Doi River Cau Mau Peninsula (Operation Seafloat)

2/17/70   RD3 Craig W. Haines, Keyser, WV—(Kien Giang Province) PCF-22 ATSB Ha Tien

5/17/70   RD3 Frederick D. Snyder, Moab, UT—(An Xugen Province) (WIA 5/16/70) PCF-64 Song Dam Doi River (Operation Seafloat)

7/6/70   QM2 Lanny H. Buroff, Chicago, IL—(An Xugen Province) PCF-40 Underwater Mine Explosion while Alongside USS Krishna ARL-30 (Operation Seafloat)

PATROL CRAFT FAST DIVISION—102 (Danang)

10/29/66 BM1 Kemper S. Billings, Burlington, NC—(Thua Thien Province) PCF-56 Lost Overboard Hue River Monsoon Surf Conditions

11/15/66 BM3 Harry G. Brock, Odessa, TX—(Thua Thien Province) PCF-77 Hue River

11/15/66 MIA RM3 Bruce A. Timmons, Ft Lauderdale, FL—(Thua Thien Province) PCF-77 Hue River

COASTAL DIVISION TWELVE (Danang)

12/6/67   BM1 Bobby D. Carver, Richmond, CA—(Quang Ngai Province) PCF-79 Sa Ky River South of Cape Batangan Peninsula

6/16/68   BM2 Anthony G. Chandler, Warner Robbins, GA—(South China Sea) PCF-19 1 ½ Miles Off Shore 5 Miles South of Ben Hai River Mouth Near the DMZ (Quang Tri Province)

6/16/68   EN2 Edward C. Cruz, Inarajan, Guam—(South China Sea) PCF-19 1 ½ Miles Off Shore 5 miles South of Ben Hai River Mouth Near the DMZ (Quang Tri Province)

6/16/68   GMG2 Billy S. Armstrong, West Helena AR—(South China Sea) PCF-19 1 ½ Miles Off Shore 5 Miles South of Ben Hai River Mouth Near the DMZ (Quang Tri Province)

6/16/68   MIA QM2 Frank Bowman, Walterboro, SC—(South China Sea) PCF-19 1 ½ Miles Off Shore 5 Miles South of Ben Hai River Mouth Near the DMZ (Quang Tri Province)

11/6/68   EN2 David L. Merrill, South Bend, IN—(South China Sea) PCF-70 Near North Side Batanga Peninsula, 64 Miles South of Chu Lai (Quang Ngai Province)

11/6/68   MIA LCPL Frederick R. Turner, Columbus, OH—(South China Sea) (USMC) MASS MSCG-18 1ˢᵗ MAW PCF-70 Passenger Near North Side Batanga Peninsula 64 Miles South of Chu Lai (Quang Ngai Province)

9/26/69   LTJG Robert L. Crosby, South Hamilton, MA—1105(Quang Nam Province) (WIA 9/24/69) Coastal Division Twelve Maintenance Officer YFNB-2, Danang

10/7/69   LTJG Kenneth D. Norton, Lady Lake, FL—1100(Quang Nam Province) OinC PCF-61 Cua Dai River

PATROL CRAFT FAST DIVISION—103(Cat Lo)

5/22/66   BM2 Raleigh L. Godley, Lawson, MO—(Phuoc Tuy Province) PCF-41 Song Dinh Ba River(Operation Jackstay-RSSZ)

COASTAL DIVISION THIRTEEN (Cat Lo)

3/11/67   SN Gary W. Friedmann, Lebanon, PA—(Phuoc Tuy Province) PCF-39 Cat Lo 81mm Mortar Double Loading Explosion During Gunnery Exercises

9/8/68   BM2 John P. McDermott, Pittsburgh, KS—(South China Sea) PCF-98 Jammed 81mm Mortar Round Misfired Alongside an LST Anchored Offshore the Ca Mau Peninsula (An Xugen Province)

12/17/68   EN2 John R. Hartkemeyer, Hamilton, OH—(An Xugen Province) PCF-51 Rach Bang Cung River (Rocket Alley) Ca Mau Peninsula (Operation Seafloat)

5/19/69   BM3 Robert A. Thompson, Downey, CA—(An Xugen Province) PCF-51 Son Bay Hap River Cau Mau Peninsula (Operation Seafloat)

10/25/70   QM1 Joseph P. Jurgella, Stevens Point, WI—(Phuoc Tuy Province) PCF-59 Cat Lo

PATROL CRAFT FAST DIVISION—105 (Qui Nhon)

10/25/66   MIA GMG3 Alvin L. Levan, Catawissa, PA—(South China Sea) PCF-87 Fell Overboard Combat Sea Patrol (Binh Dinh Province)

COASTAL DIVISION FIFTEEN (Qui Nhon)

3/29/67   GMGSN Dennis R. Puckett, Lee Summit, MO—(South China Sea) PCF-63 Fell Overboard Combat Sea Patrol (Binh Dinh Province)

11/29/67   LTJG William H. Murphy III, Madison, WI—1100(Thua Thien Province) UH-1C Passenger USA A/1/9th CAV A Shau Valley

12/23/67   EN2 Carl R. Goodfellow, Waterproof, LA—(Bing Dinh Province) PCF-88 Det-Qui Nhon Sapper Attack at Barracks

11/8/68   LTJG Richard C. Wallace, Norfolk, VA—1105(South China Sea) PCF-89 Accidental 81mm Mortar Explosion Combat Sea Patrol (Binh Dinh Province)

11/8/68   BM3 Peter P. Blasko Jr., Southern Pines, NC—(South China Sea) PCF-89 Accidental 81mm Mortar Explosion Combat Sea Patrol (Binh Dinh Province)

11/8/68   BM3 Stephen T. Volz, Lakewood, CA—(South China Sea) PCF-89 Accidental 81mm Mortar Explosion Combat Sea Patrol (Binh Dinh Province)

6/22/69   RD2 Kenneth P. West, Butte, MT—(Gia Dinh Province) In Transit NSA Saigon Det-Nha Be Fell off Ammi Pontoon Nha Be Navy Pier Soi Rap River

7/2/69   MIA EN3 Albert M. Fransen Jr., Las Vegas, NV—(South China Sea) PCF-87 Qui Nhon 81mm Mortar Accident Combat Sea Patrol (Binh Dinh Province)

7/2/69   GMG3 Glen C. Keene Jr., Fairhope, AL—(South China Sea) PCF-87 Qui Nhon 81mm Mortar Accident Combat Sea Patrol (Binh Dinh Province)

CHAPTER ONE

Market Time: The Mission

O peration Market Time: its mission was to stop the infiltration of men and material by sea along the entire South Vietnamese coastline; to provide gunfire support to friendly ground units; and to provide psychological warfare operations as needed.

A system of patrol areas was set up to enforce the security of the South Vietnamese coastline and to deny them to the enemy. Since the majority of friendly commerce moved by water using the coastline intermingling with a large commercial fishing industry, the problem of detecting enemy movement mixed with the friendly watercraft became a complicated task. This was an advantage, which the enemy exploited, in the early days of the war.

The patrol areas extended from the Demilitarized Zone at the North and South Vietnamese border all the way south, around the Ca Mau Peninsula and then northwest to the Cambodian border. PCF's also known as Swift Boats were assigned to areas from the coastline to approximately two miles out to sea. For each two Swift Boat patrol areas, covering the waters from two to four miles out, U.S Coast Guard WPB patrol boats were assigned. For each two WPB areas, a U.S. Navy destroyer or USCG High Endurance Cutter (WHEC) was assigned covering the waters from four to twelve miles out. These larger vessels were used to monitor and even to board and search the larger steel hull junks and merchant ships that appeared to be on a suspicious mission. Working with the U.S. Navy P-3 Orion tracker aircraft, they could cover large distances and remain on station for several weeks at a time. These vessels were also used as mother ships for the smaller patrol craft enabling them to remain on station longer thereby avoiding the long transit distances from their home bases.

Swift Boats were a unique type of patrol boat and it was their uniqueness that made them special to the mission and their crews. They were 50 feet long with a welded aluminum hull powered by twin Detroit Diesels that generated 450 horsepower. An Onan Generator gave them A/C power for radios, boarding lights and for the refrigerator/freezer. Five bunks were used for sleeping while off watch but the small size of the boat prohibited living on board for extended lengths of time.

Armament consisted of twin 50 Caliber machine guns on top
81 MM direct fire mortar with a single 50 Cal machine gun mou
style rounding out the main battery. Small arms, an M-79 grenade l
an M-60 machine gun for the peak tank in the bow made the Swif
armed gunboat capable of a variety of missions.

Unlike other gunboats such as the PBR and the river assault group
assigned specific ratings which were cross-trained to know each oth
submarine crewmen. The ratings were (1) A junior officer, LTJG or Ens
Mate, (3) Radarman, (4) Quartermaster, (5) Boatswains Mate, (6) E
Engineman was required to be an EN2 or EN1 whereas the other rating coul
grade. Since the crew's lives depended on the power plant and electrical
boat, a senior petty officer was required for the Engineer.

The senior enlisted crewman was designated the Leading Petty Officer
in command to the Officer in Charge of the crew. Since the Engineman was
EN1, he became the LPO on most crews since he was senior. Also because En
typically work in the engine room of a ship and rarely handle guns or see com
provided a radically different environment for these petty officers. I must add
prejudice intended that most of these enginemen rose to the challenge and serve
capacity proudly.

The patrols were usually twenty-four hours in length with most of the crew up
about during the day and split up into two watch sections at night. The OinC headed on
section and the other was headed by the LPO.

The home bases for these boats were called Coastal Divisions and were numbered 11
12, 13, 14, and 15. These divisions were based at An Thoi, DaNang, Cat Lo, Cam Rahn Bay,
and Qui Nhon, respectively. Repair and support facilities in the form of repair ships or
repair shops and living quarters on barges were built at each home base. Some of the
bases had barracks built ashore as the bases were developed into more modern facilities.

Patrol schedules were set giving each crew a twenty-four hour patrol, one day on and
one day off. Depending on the patrol schedule, the one day off could be non-existent.
For example: Areas farthest away from the home base departed between 0400 and 0600.
A crew could return from a patrol area far from the home base late in the day and after
cleanup and scheduled maintenance, i.e. oil changes, refueling and rearming of the
boat, have very little free time left until going on patrol again the next day. This free time
was for rest, to go to the exchange or to the club for a few beers, or even a USO Show if
there was one scheduled.

A typical Market Time Patrol begins when the crew boards the boat they are assigned
for that patrol. Each crewmember checks out his assigned area and equipment. Even
though the boat designated for the days patrol is assigned to the crew as "their boat", a
thorough checkout must still be done in case another crew had used their boat for a patrol
or the repair staff had performed repairs and service.

Ammunition and spares are checked, fuel and oil levels as well as spare water and oil
cans are checked, radios and radio checks are performed, charts and up to date intelligence

for the area is located and stored, lines and safety gear is checked and all loose gear is properly secured for sea in case of heavy weather. By the time all checks have been performed, the OinC comes aboard bringing the pubs, codebooks, and challenge/reply codes for the days of the patrol. The LPO reports, "The crew is ready to get underway" to the OinC and lines are cast off to get underway. The boat proceeds to the APL to pick up the food rations for the patrol. While many thought we lived off C-rations, we in fact loaded chicken, steak, pork chops, bacon and eggs, canned goods, ingredients for sandwiches, fruit, milk and cheese. One of the crewmen was the designated "cook" and he was responsible for getting the food the crew liked and being a good "diplomat" in the galley was very helpful. Once the food is stored, we get underway and proceed out the harbor. In DaNang, a stop was made at the South Vietnamese Navy Pier to pick up our liaison/interpreter. Just behind their quarters was CSC or Coastal Surveillance Center. The OinC walked to CSC to pick up the latest intelligence and special assignments for the patrol area we had been assigned. When he returned, we got underway and proceeded out the harbor heading north or south whichever direction the patrol area was located.

As we proceed out of the harbor of DaNang, one cannot help but observe the bustling activity in this busy harbor. Large merchant ships and smaller Naval cargo vessels and LST's carry supplies and material into and out of DaNang. Fuel, ammunition, food, spare parts, vehicles, artillery weapons, and building materials are brought in from the U.S. and other ports. Most of these are unloaded at the Deepwater Piers and LST Ramps near Monkey Mountain. These supplies are taken by truck to Naval Support Activity, DaNang supply centers for redistribution to the fighting men in the field.

Most of the supplies are sent to firebases and support facilities throughout the I Corps area. Some of the supplies are loaded aboard smaller Naval Craft such as LCU's, YFU's and YOG's for fuel. These craft proceed out of the harbor to destinations along the coast such as Chu Lai, Cua Viet, Tam My, and Wonder Beach, including the many Coastal Groups that support the Naval Advisors for the Vietnamese Junk Force.

As we move toward our patrol area, we travel among these supply craft as they ply the same waters delivering their vital cargoes. Passing them, enroute to our assigned area, we watch the hundreds of South Vietnamese Junks and Sampans weave in and out of the columns of Naval Craft as they travel to fishing grounds or deliver their cargos of rice, nhuc mom, lumber and other supplies for the Vietnamese people. Sometimes, it can get pretty crowded entering and leaving a busy harbor like DaNang.

Soon, we begin to establish radio contact with the boat we are to relieve on station and they begin to travel south toward us. Radio messages give our location using code names for the river mouths and peninsula's jutting out from the coastline.

"Newsboy India 69, this is Newsboy India 12, over". We use Newsboy India and the boat number so the Viet Cong do not know which patrol area is being relieved.

"Newsboy India 12, this is Newsboy India 69, do you copy?" comes the reply. "Newsboy India 69, I copy, interrogative your latest??" "Newsboy India 12, my latest Marlboro plus two." This means PCF-69 is two miles north of Chon May Point, a peninsula just north of DaNang that uses a code name of any cigarette.

And so it goes, until the two boats meet and come alongside each other. Information is passed, such as the latest intelligence on the area, the level of enemy activity and junk traffic. All this is shared with the oncoming PCF. Once this is finished, the two crews part company and one heads for home as fast as they can while the other proceeds to its patrol area and assumes the call sign of the area, i.e. Enfield Cobra Charlie Mike.

Once on station, we begin to check out the area for boat traffic and look for suspicious looking junks and sampans. Sometimes while proceeding toward a group of fishing sampans, one will break off and head away from the group. Immediately, the crew springs to Action Stations, the engines roar to life, and the fighting Swift heads for the evading sampan. A siren whines out its call to stop and the wise Vietnamese turns away from the beach. Maneuvering alongside, weapons at the ready, the crew searches the sampan while the liaison/interpreter checks the boats papers and the identification cards of the fisherman. Most end up being scared fisherman with papers in order. To them, we supply a packet of fishhooks, band-aids, tobacco and papers, along with some leaflets in Vietnamese looking for information on the Viet Cong and their movements. The sampan is cast off and moves on its way usually with smiles and a wave of the hand.

Sometimes, however, the sampan or junk doesn't stop and continues to evade toward the beach. Under the rules of engagement, the sampan can now be pursued and taken under fire if necessary. The PCF, now in hot pursuit, bears down on the fleeing sampan, at battle stations, weapons ready. Sometimes, though not often, small arms fire will erupt from the sampan especially if the distance to the beach and safety is extensive. Given a choice, the Viet Cong will run rather than to fight a Swift Boat in the open sea. The job of the Swift Boat is to cut down the distance quickly and at 28 knots, adrenaline pumping, the machine guns begin to fire at the shoreline to cut off the escape. If the Viet Cong suspects open fire, the Swift Boat answers with deadly accuracy and the battle is quickly over. One of the dangers is that the Swift Boat can be drawn into an ambush close to shore as the fleeing sampan lures it into rocket or recoilless rifle range. This means the crewmembers not involved in firing weapons must be alert and aware of their surroundings at all time. Once the fleeing suspects are stopped or killed, a thorough search of the sampan for contraband and papers or documents to see what it was that the suspects were afraid of being captured with. This information is used in a radio message to CSC DaNang called a "spot report", giving location, details of the pursuit, ammunition expended and casualties, both enemy and friendly.

Then it is back to patrolling the area. Sometimes a crew can spend several patrols without any incident and then find one that explodes in a firefight. Firefights can last from a few minutes to an hour or more depending on the Viet Cong's position and willingness to fight. A wise OinC will analyze the situation and decide whether to stand and fight or withdraw to the open sea and call for assistance. This assistance can be in the form of Coast Guard or Navy Ships nearby, air support, the neighboring Swift Boats on patrol, or even Marine or Army Artillery Gunfire. All of these are available and are used to assist the Swift Boat on patrol in case of engagement with a larger enemy force. Knowing the capabilities of these assets and how to call them for support is the mark of an experienced and capable Swift Boat Officer and crew.

As the routine of the patrol settles in, the boat traffic subsides and the crewmember that does the cooking begins to prepare the evening meal. A hot plate and electric frying pan are his only tools but it still makes for an enjoyable meal. Fried chicken, green beans, salad with tomatoes and cucumbers, boiled potatoes, bread and butter are prepared as well as can be under the weather conditions. But it looks and tastes very good and much better than C-rations. We eat in shifts maintaining our position in the patrol area.

Darkness begins to fall and the OinC is on the radio communicating with shore units to set up some harassment and interdiction fire targets for after dark. These are usually Viet Cong trails and assembly points and carefully checked to make certain that no friendly units will be affected by the fire. This also establishes communications with these shore units to enable us to be in position to assist them with support fire from our mortar for any nighttime operations or sweeps of the area. This completed, the crew splits up into two watches beginning at 2200. One section, led by the OinC, will man the helm and the lookout in the gun tub. The other section is led by the LPO. The Vietnamese Liaison/interpreter remains available in the main cabin when needed and does not stand a watch.

With one section on watch, the others turn in to the bunks for some rest, although ready for any emergency. Sometime around midnight, during the watch change, the guns are manned and mortar rounds are readied for the firing mission. The boat moves into position for the firing mission. The mortar is locked at 090 or 270 relative and then is locked at the proper altitude setting. The Quartermaster takes his position fixes from a point or river mouth and draws a 90-degree arc on the chart. This gives him the heading, which gives the least roll factor with the stern to the sea. When the boat is in position, the command to open fire is given by the OinC and round after round is dropped into the tube. Usually a mission of ten to twelve rounds of high explosive mixed with one or two white phosphorous rounds are fired if the shore units monitor the mission. The 81 MM mortar has a range of nearly two miles over relatively flat terrain. Firing mission over, the off watch turns in for some rest.

Thus it goes through the night with the helm watching the radar for contacts and the lookout watching for lighted watercraft moving at night. The watches include checks of engines and electronics in service.

Morning arrives with the smell of bacon and hot coffee filling the cabin. Logs are updated and preparations to be relieved are begun, the boat is cleaned up and gear stowed for the transit back to base. Each crewmember checks his equipment and area for problems that need to be corrected either by the repair staff or the crew upon return to base. Ammunition is inventoried and these lists are given to the LPO to coordinate these efforts. By using this method, the cleanup time can be reduced so the remaining time can be used for personal business and a hot shower or even a trip to the EM club for a beer or two.

We move toward the southern part of our area and wait for the call from our relieving Swift Boat on its way to our area. Sometimes a Navy Ship is offshore in our area and we make a trip out to check her out. Going alongside the ship gives the ships crew a chance to take pictures of a small combatant on patrol. It gives the OinC a chance to go aboard and chat with the skipper of the ship and the crew can use the ships store if possible. Blue Dungarees are the uniform worn by Swift Boat Sailors and the laundry is very hard on them. Getting replacements is a welcome opportunity for all of us. Usually the ship shares its stores of fresh fruit and even ice cream with us as well. The OinC returns with fresh intelligence and the ship gains a new respect for these small combat craft making up the inshore line of Market Time. We shove off from the ship giving the crew one last chance for pictures or 8 MM movies as we move back on station.

Suddenly, the radio crackles with the call, "Newsboy India 12 this is Newsboy India 56, do you copy, over?" Our reply goes out to our relief and we head toward a rendezvous.

Arriving at the rendezvous, the two Swift Boats exchange information, followed by separation with one boat heading on station and the other heading back to base. The cycle continues for another day.

We stop at CSC to drop off our liaison/interpreter, and proceed to the base. After stopping to refuel the boat, we move to the pier to rearm the boat, replacing ammunition used on patrol. Then it is over to the nest of Swift Boats to clean up, change oil if necessary, weapons are cleaned, spaces are scrubbed down, paint is touched up, and gear is stowed away. When all work is done, the crew heads for the barracks ship and a hot shower and chow. The OinC checks in with the Coastal Division 12 Staff and files his after action reports, if any. He gets our patrol assignment for the next day and relays it to the LPO and the crew. If there are repairs needed on the boat by the shops, the crewmember will return to coordinate these repairs on the boat.

Meanwhile, back on station, the Swift Boats, the Coast Guard WPB's and the Naval Ships, assisted by P-2 Orion Aircraft, continue the patrols all up and down the coastline of South Vietnam. Market Time is the name of the operation, and CTF-115 Headquartered in Cam Rahn Bay is responsible for its execution.

CHAPTER TWO

Training For The Mission

Training for this mission begins in Coronado, California, near San Diego. Here, the officers and enlisted men are formed into crews to be trained as a unit and sent in country to serve together. It consists of a week of indoctrination classes on Vietnam, its culture, and the part that Market Time plays in the war theatre. This is followed by a week of survival training culminating in SERE, Survival, Evasion Resistance and Escape. This includes a training session at a mock POW camp in Warner Springs, CA. It is very intensive and designed to prepare us for the probability that we can be captured and interred in a POW Camp. We learn the tools of survival and resistance in a prisoner of war situation. The next six weeks consists of training on the Swift Boats themselves and their mission. Some of the training takes place with the crew together, while other training required the crew to be split up as the officers and quartermasters attended Vietnamese Language School, the enginemen learned all about the engines and related electrical, plumbing and fuel systems aboard the Swift Boat. The Radarmen spend time with the Electronic Technicians to learn the radar and radio systems. The Gunners mates learn the techniques of operating and repair of the three Browning 50 Caliber Machine Guns, the M-60 Machine Gun, the 81 MM Mortar and the various small arms carried aboard a Swift Boat. Cleaning and maintenance of the gun mounts and the ammunition used aboard the boat are taught in detail. Boatswain Mates learn boat handling skills and proper preservation and maintenance of the aluminum hulled Swift Boat. Toward the end of the training, the crews are sent to 29 Palms Marine Base for heavy weapons training. Returning to the base, the crew attends classes that give each man some knowledge of all the systems and equipment for cross training of each rating. Knowing everyone's job is essential for survival of this small crew on the Swift Boat. In case of a casualty to one of the crew, someone else can fill in enabling the crew to get out of a hot situation. Some of the crews were put together short of one or more ratings due to manning levels making this cross training even more important. Sometimes a Boatswains Mate becomes an engineer or a Radarman becomes a Quartermaster. Inasmuch as possible, the crews are outfitted with the correct ratings although sometimes this is not completed until they arrive in country.

The last part of the training involves actual board and search exercises between Swift Boats and Vietnamese Junks off the coast of California in daytime and night exercises. Having graduated this course of training, the crews are shipped to Vietnam arriving first in Cam Rahn Bay, home to the headquarters of Market Time and Coastal Squadron One.

In my particular case, the training was somewhat different. Assembled in Coronado were several Junior Officers slated to be OinC's, a Quartermaster, a Gunners mate, and thirteen Enginemen, all EN2's and EN1's. With no group of other ratings in the pipeline, a decision was made to train the enginemen as a group and send us in country as replacements. There had been a period prior to this time, April 1968, when there was a shortage of enginemen and it was decided that we were needed as soon as possible. Our training was different than as a crew but it gave us much more time with the engines and electrical systems of the Swift Boat. This proved to be a real plus when we arrived in country and joined crews without engineers.

In our training classes, we learned to navigate, to field strip and setup the heavy weapons. We disassembled the training engines completely and reassembled them, started them up and let the staff try to trick us by making casualties to the engines such as loss of oil pressure, overheating, clogged fuel lines, etc. These were invaluable to us and we learned much information about our jobs aboard the new boats. I felt sorry for the QMCS that tried to teach thirteen engineers how to navigate but he did a tremendous job nonetheless. We did not get language training, did not go to 29 Palms for weapons training, but received instruction on the radios, radar, and antenna tuning skills that we would not have received.

Very soon, it was graduation time and we boarded the aircraft for McCord Air Force Base in Washington State. We had no orders and did not know our ultimate destinations, so instead we were sent to Cam Rahn Bay. It was a long tiring flight on a chartered airliner, but after stops in Alaska, Japan, and Okinawa for fuel we arrived in Cam Rahn Bay. We received indoctrination by the U.S. Air Force at the terminal and then a short ride by truck over the mountain to the Market Time Base. The humidity and heat hit us like a hammer as we left the aircraft and then again as we left the air-conditioned terminal.

The Market Time Base was the Headquarters of Coastal Squadron One and Coastal Division 14. Some of us would end up staying right there depending on our orders. We were given bunks in the barracks for the night and after stowing our gear, headed off to the EM Club for a few drinks and our last night together as a group. We had become very close, almost like a large crew but soon we would become a part of a seasoned crew at our new destination. We talked about what this would be like, joining a crew that had no engineer and how we would fit in. Other crews had trained together and we did not. It was something that only happened once during the war and we were it. We wondered how many of us would survive the war, how we would react in our first fire fight, and toasted to our brotherhood vowing to meet again after we returned from our tour on Swift Boats. Being E-5 and E-6, some of us would end up as LPO's on seasoned crews and we discussed what that would be like. Knowing that the Chain of Command was in place, we felt it would not be a problem but yet it was a source of stress for us coming into a seasoned crew. One thing that we agreed on, we had received the finest training on this equipment that the

Navy could provide and it was up to us to use it to provide a valuable asset to whatever crew we were assigned.

We toasted once more to our success and good luck to each other, and then returned to the barracks for good nights sleep. Apprehension of what was to come and the jet lag kept most of us up late but soon we fell asleep.

Reveille came early and we packed our gear and headed for breakfast. At 0800, we mustered outside Coastal Squadron One Headquarters and were briefed by the staff yeoman. He then posted the assignments on the bulletin board for us to read. Since we were all the same ratings, he gave us 30 minutes to check over the list and swap assignments so buddies could be together if we wanted. I was assigned with three other Enginemen to DaNang. I remembered from my training that DaNang was in I Corps to the north and the quarters were two APL's or living barges. Air Conditioning, after a night in the hot humid barracks, made it sound very welcome indeed. With our gear in hand, we gathered near the truck again for the drive back to the Air Base and the flights to our new assignments. We said goodbye to those staying in Cam Rahn Bay and climbed aboard the truck. At the Air Base Terminal, we separated again as some of us went to Coastal Division 11 at An Thoi, Coastal Division 13 at Cat Lo, Coastal Division 15 at Qui Nhon, and Coastal Division 12 at DaNang.

For four of the Enginemen, EN1 Terry S. Johnson, EN2 Stanley J. DeMerchant, EN2 Raymond W. Nix, and myself, EN2 James W. Steffes, it was a short flight to DaNang Air Base to the north. We had departed the United States on June 3rd and arrived at our assigned Coastal Divisions on June 6th, 1968. An assignment unlike anything this group of Enginemen had experienced was about to begin.

CHAPTER THREE

The Mission Begins

We arrived at DaNang Air Base aboard a C-130 Cargo Aircraft filled with men from all branches of the services, Army, Navy, Marines and Air Force most of them in green fatigues. We were wearing blue dungarees which made us stand out from the others on the aircraft but it was much cooler than the wool dress blues we wore when we arrived at Cam Rahn Bay. Stepping out of the aircraft, we were met with the same, slap in the face, hot humid climate as Cam Rahn Bay. It seemed different, somehow, a little less humid maybe, and a feeling of danger that I did not sense in Cam Rahn Bay. I wondered how my fellow Enginemen felt as they disembarked from similar aircraft at the other Swift Base locations. We grabbed our sea bags and other luggage from the tarmac and moved along in single file toward the terminal. Everywhere we looked, were row after row of green aircraft of all types. There were jet fighters taking off and landing on the runway we had just landed in on making deafening sound to our ears. Rows of cargo planes and some helicopters lined the tarmac on which we stood. I learned later that most of the helicopters and other aircraft were nearby at the Marble Mountain Air Base.

We filed into the terminal and were directed to an assembly area near a canteen. Having converted our greenback dollars to Military Payment Certificates (MPC) for short, we made our first purchases of cold sodas while we waited for a ride to our new home. As we sat and pondered our new environment, the vast expanse of war equipment and the orderliness of it all made us stare in awe and realize how small an item we really are.

Very soon, we spotted a man dressed like us in blue dungarees and he headed in our direction.

"Welcome to Vietnam!!!" he yelled and we immediately felt welcome. "Grab your gear and follow me," he ordered.

We picked up our gear and followed him to a strange looking vehicle. It was a tractor-trailer, but the trailer looked more like a large horse trailer. It was low to the ground and an open door in the side led to benches and poles to hold on to. We tossed our gear inside on the floor and our guide told us it was call a cattle hauler. The name fit somehow, and soon we were on our way to the Small Boat Base near Monkey Mountain. Traveling along a dusty road with red clay dust blowing everywhere. We watched the scenery move by the windows, everything from concertina wire and fenced compounds, to mud huts with thatched roofs and dirty water in rice paddies. After a thirty-minute ride or so, we turned into a long road that led to a waterfront area. The truck stopped in front of a pier with two large APL's or living barges and the YR-71, which is a repair barge. Two Swift Boats were sitting on skids on the pier between the barges and to the left was a stretch of land with several LCU's or Landing Craft Utility. We disembarked, grabbed our gear and headed for the office of Coastal Division 12 on board the YR-71. Outboard the YR-71 were numerous Swift Boats nested together in groups of four. They sure looked good sitting there and we wondered which one each of us would finally serve aboard.

We entered the office of the Division Commander, LT Ian M. Bailey, where EN1 Terry Smith presented our orders and introduced us. Mr. Bailey welcomed us warmly and asked us how our flight was and our reactions to Vietnam. He then made a phone call to the APL's wardroom asking for several officers to come to the office. Our records were turned over to the Yeoman and we waited for the officers to arrive. A tall, Ltjg, Peter Snyder was the first to arrive and looked at us kind of funny.

Lt Bailey said to him, "Mr. Snyder, you have a new snipe, EN2 Steffes." I stepped forward and shook his hand. He gripped my hand and said to Lt. Bailey, "Really, my own snipe, honest?" I felt somewhat strange but his smile wiped out the anxiety that I felt and we stepped outside to get acquainted. I told him we were part of a class of thirteen Engineman that had trained together in Coronado and were not part of any crews. The course was modified to fit our unique group and although we did not get any underway training on a Swift Boat, we did receive extensive training on the engines and boat systems. He said, "Great, because I have been using a Second Class Boatswains Mate for an engineer." His crew had been in country for a little over two months and had yet to take charge of his own boat. "We have to have an engineer to get our own boat," he explained. He went on to explain that his crew was going on patrol in about two hours and I should get ready to go. He stuck his head in the office and told Lt Bailey that he would be taking me right away. I asked about "break in patrols" and he replied that he would "break me in". Lt Bailey said that was fine with him and he closed the door. "Break in patrols" were normally assigned to new crews by splitting them up among experienced crews for several patrols to "learn the ropes" before going on their own. Since we were not in a crew, Ltjg Snyder felt it was unnecessary to do this and he would put me in the crew right away. He told me to follow him and leave my gear in the office until tomorrow morning and take some cigarettes and a jacket if I needed it. The mission was the Echo Night Patrol, an area just outside the DaNang Harbor that was manned only at night from 1600 to 0700.

I followed him to the side of the YR-71 where the rest of the crew was already aboard a Swift Boat getting ready to take it out on patrol. He called the crew together to meet me and told a Seaman to report to the office. I was greeted with smiles and handshakes from the crew. These guys looked like seasoned veterans compared to me but they welcomed me none the less.

Figure 1. The Crew of PCF-12 in 1968. I am in the front row, right side.

First was QM3 Gary Rosenberger, our Quartermaster from Baltimore, Maryland. Next was GMGSN Tom Klemash, our Gunners mate from South Carolina. Next to introduce himself was RD3 Kenneth Bloch, our Radarman from Minnesota. Great, my home state, as we shared hometown names, I felt a bond with him right away. He explained that he was also our cook, a job he performed besides caring for our radios and radar equipment. Last but not least, BM2 Johnnie Fitts, from Missouri, our Boatswains Mate and Leading Petty Officer. Mr. Snyder explained that Fitts was in charge of the crew, second in command to him, and the gunner on the after mount, an 81 MM Mortar with a 50 Cal Machine Gun on top. I would be his loader when the Swift Boat Guns were manned.

With the introductions finished, we all turned to our respective tasks, getting the Swift Boat ready to go on patrol. Guns were checked, radios and radar checked, deck gear stowed, charts for the patrol area, and of course the engines. I checked fluid levels in the engines, spare oil and water in cans, loose gear in the engine room and lazarette, fuel level in the tanks, fresh water, valve lineup for fuel tanks, all routine for me. I felt good about the status of the engines and when ready, I started them up, started the Onan Generator and unhooked the electric cable from shore power. As each of us reported ready to get underway, the lines were cast off and we proceeded to the APL to pick up chow for the patrol. We tied up to the APL and waited for Bloch to come back from the galley with tonight's supplies for supper. I was eager for my first patrol and nervous at the same time. Everyone said it would be just routine, easy for them to say, they had done this before.

I remained topside as the Swift Boat moved away from the APL and turned its bow toward the harbor entrance. I enjoyed the wind in my face and watched the scenery go by, wondering whom and where the enemy was hiding. How would I react to my first firefight? What would I do if we had an engine casualty while engaged with the enemy? How long would a fire fight last? Would this crew accept me? All of these things ran through my mind as we moved ever closer to the open sea.

CHAPTER FOUR

First Patrol

The Swift Boat stopped at an empty pier near the Coastal Surveillance Center. A South Vietnamese Sailor climbed aboard and introduced himself as Phoung. He was our interpreter and always went on patrol with our crew. His family lived near Hue and his English was pretty good. His job was to speak to the fishermen and interpret their papers. Each Vietnamese carried his own ID card and the boats had papers. These had to be checked and although we had been trained to look for proper papers, only these guys could tell the fakes from the real ones. Mr. Snyder walked up to the CSC to get the latest intelligence and code books for the Echo Patrol Area. He returned shortly and without delay we cast off the lines and headed for our operating area.

A short high speed run to the harbor entrance showed the Swift Boat had some spunk and I felt the surge of power under my feet as the boat sped across the waves.

We approached some small sampans entering the harbor and as Gary Rosenberger steered the boat toward them, he pushed the button that made the siren on the top of the cabin wail its warning tone. I went up to the pilothouse and Mr. Snyder informed me that we were going to search this watercraft. My job was to stand clear with an M-16 rifle and watch the crew at work. The sampans came alongside and tied up with their lines. One man was in the gun tub, one was steering from the after helm, one man manning the radios, and the rest of us stood on the rear of the boat. Phoung came topside and reached for the papers handed to him by the fisherman. It was very sad, they looked so poor, clothes were ragged, and the boat looked barely seaworthy. I watched as the crew ordered the fishermen to open up the covers in the boat, open baskets containing fish, other containers held rice and other supplies. They looked frightened but Phoung soon put them at ease as he handed their papers back. All was in order and Johnnie Fitts handed them packets containing fishhooks, line, and some tobacco and papers. Fitts explained that these were Psy-ops packages, designed to help the fishermen and make friends with them. Some government literature was included to enlist the help of these fishermen in identifying Viet Cong infiltrators and giving us information on their activities in their villages and fishing grounds.

With all things in order, we cast off the sampan and it proceeded on its way. I was able to ask questions but it seemed pretty straightforward and simple. Mr. Snyder explained that being vigilant was very important and the enemy used the fisherman by moving among them as they infiltrated supplies and arms into the south. Any fisherman with bogus papers or carrying too much rice or suspicious bundles must be taken seriously. He explained that we also boarded and searched boats and junks at night using our board and searchlights and I should check them out before dark to make sure they are working properly. They operated off the Onan Generator.

Mr. Snyder called in to CSC DaNang, call sign "Article" to report that we were on station and assumed the call sign "Enfield Cobra Echo". The Swift Boat moved north through the "Gap" and into the bay that made up the patrol area "Echo". The crew settled into the routine of watching for boat traffic, while Ken Bloch started cooking supper. For the rest of the evening, Enfield Cobra Echo patrolled this large bay stopping and searching several sampans and one large cargo junk. As darkness closed in, we turned off the lights and half the crew lay down to catch a few winks of sleep always ready for any emergency.

Enfield Cobra Echo is a relatively quiet patrol area, turns out to be a good one for me to learn the ropes on. We contacted an Army Fire Base on the beach area and received some H&I, (H&I stands for "Harassment and Interdiction"), targets for later firing. Usually, the crew would get up around midnight and fire several rounds into these coordinates, which are suspected VC infiltration routes. The purpose is to keep the VC off balance and possibly cause a few casualties to the enemy.

So it happened then, that at the turn of the watch around midnight, our crew moved into position and fired 10 rounds of 81MM, high explosive mortar rounds onto Chon May Point, a peninsula that made up the northern edge of our patrol area. I remembered my training well and the loading of the mortar rounds went well. I then stood the midnight to 0200 watch with BM2 Fitts, taking turns at the wheel and up on lookout in the gun tub. I observed many flares and blinking lights from aircraft along with red streams of tracer fire leading to the ground. It certainly looked like a war going on from where I sat. Sometime around 0400, as I got up for my watch again, loud booming sounds coming from the beach area meant the Army was firing its artillery for someone in trouble. We stood two hours on and two hours off watch during the night and found my mind wandering to the danger posed by the noises of war in the night. Somehow, I fell asleep in the bunk down in the forward compartment. Soon it was time to go on watch again at 0400. I was in the gun tub when the sun began to rise in the east. The fishing boat traffic was already underway from the DaNang harbor heading toward the rising sun. The patrol was nearly over and I went down to wake the rest of the crew. I checked my engines once again and as the crew arose, cleanup began in earnest. The Echo patrol area had no relief on station so we proceeded into the harbor. A stop at the Vietnamese Navy Pier to drop off Phoung and turn in the pubs to CSC, took a few minutes and then it was full speed to the nest of Swift Boats tied up to YR-71. I felt sticky and needed a shower which made the gray barracks ship look very inviting. I looked forward to getting my gear stowed in a locker and finding my own bunk. We still had work to do, as I was about to find out.

We tied up to the pier where we took on ammunition to replace what we had fired and then over to the YR-71 location of the fueling hose. I topped off the fuel tanks and fresh water. We moved the boat to the nest and I hooked up shore power followed by securing the engines and Onan generator. As each of us began our checkout and cleanup duties, I talked to BM2 Fitts about the engine logs and where I would get the oil and water to replenish the cans stored on deck. I checked all my levels and filled up the engines with oil and water as needed. A quick wipe down of the engines and then asked if I could help anyone else. Before we left the boat, Ltjg Snyder took a look around the boat and asked me if I had any questions. He assigned Fitts to assist me in getting my gear over to the APL and checked in properly. I had to get sheets, blankets, drop off my records at personnel and then get cleaned up.

As I went to all the places to check in, I got a shot from sickbay that was forgotten, issued malaria pills, and found out how we get paid. I reminded Personnel that although I was on an extension of my enlistment, it had not started yet so I could re-enlist anytime up to July 11th. It was decided that July 6th would do just fine and the papers would be drawn up. Hopefully the patrol schedule would allow this to happen. From there I proceeded to the berthing area and met HM1 Wood, the Master at Arms. He assigned me a bunk, a locker, and issued bedding to me. Fitts left me alone to get squared away, showed me where the rest of the crew slept, and said we could go over to the club later for a beer or two. Our next patrol would be tomorrow and he would let me know as soon as he found out. He explained that the boats assigned to different patrol areas departed at different times depending on the transit distance.

I ended my second day in Vietnam with a couple beers at the EM Club in Camp Tien Sha and crawled into my bunk where I slept soundly for the first time in several days.

CHAPTER FIVE

On Patrol June 5, 1968

My third day in DaNang began early as I climbed out of my bunk and looked around at my new home. The berthing compartment had canvas bunks rigged five high, was cramped, but it was air-conditioned. With the outside temperature in the 90's, it certainly felt good to me. I dressed and headed for the mess decks for breakfast. There I found the rest of the crew known as Crew "F", filling up on eggs and bacon. BM2 Johnnie Fitts informed me that we would be leaving at 0900 for patrol area Delta, north of DaNang and gave me the number of the boat.

I finished my meal and headed for the berthing compartment to pick up some gear for the patrol. This being my first full patrol, I wasn't certain what to bring, so I packed a change of clothes, a book, cigarettes, and my shaving kit. I took my working jacket just in case the weather turned colder up north. It turned out that my instincts were correct and I had packed the right things.

I proceeded to the boat we were assigned for this patrol and dropped my bag in the forward compartment. The rest of the crew was already hard at work checking out the boat. Normally the crew that used the boat last would have cleaned it, rearmed, and refueled it when they came in. Whoever owned this boat would have the day off since we were using their boat. I dropped into the engine room and began my engine checks, made sure that I found the tools and the spare oil and water cans were full and secured on deck. This being done, I looked around to see if I could help someone else get ready. I felt welcome among these veterans but felt apprehensive for the moment of our first engagement with the enemy and how I would fit in. Maybe our Skipper would hold drills or something, I could only hope. In the meantime, I knew that my engine room was ready and started them up to listen to the sounds of the powerful Detroit Diesel 12V71 engines. All sounded good and as the engines warmed up, the Skipper came aboard. We all reported ready to get underway and he headed for the pilothouse to stow his gear.

QM3 Gary Rosenberger eased the PCF away from the nest and headed for the APL to pick up chow for the patrol. Once alongside, RD3 Ken Bloch climbed aboard to pick up the food and supplies for the patrol. When he returned we all pitched in to bring it all aboard. We had enough for lunch on the way, a dinner while on station, and breakfast in the morning. There was also lunchmeat, bread, potato chips and stuff to munch on between meals. Ken Bloch informed us that we would have fried chicken and mashed potatoes, gravy, and green beans for dinner. What a feast!!!! Once the supplies were loaded, Gary Rosenberger moved the boat out into the harbor and on to the South Vietnamese Navy Base to pick up our interpreter. Everything seemed to be according to a plan and I was feeling very good about this duty.

A stop at the Vietnamese pier to pick up Phoung, pubs for the patrol area and any intelligence we needed to know for this patrol. This could include operations and or major troop movements and naval ships operating in our area for the next 24 hours.

With all aboard, we headed north into a brisk breeze and a light chop on the water. I stood on deck and smelled the salt air as we cleared the harbor entrance. The crew moved inside the cabin as the PCF moved through the "Gap" and headed north. The Gap is a narrow passage between a large rock and the point where snipers have known to take pot shots at Swift Boats moving through this spot. This time there were no shots and we moved northward increasing speed in the calm waters. We crossed the bay, which is the "Echo Night" patrol area, and I watched as now familiar landscape moved by our port side. As we approached the first major peninsula jutting out into the South China Sea, Mr. Snyder explained the transit coding system to me.

While we were transiting to our patrol area, our call sign would be "Newsboy India XX" with the XX being the number of the PCF. As we proceeded northward, a call on the radio to the boat we are to relieve would sound like this:

"Enfield Cobra Delta, Enfield Cobra Delta, this is Newsboy India XX, do you copy, over"

This call would go out until we received a response. The response would go like this:

"Newsboy India XX, Newsboy India XX, this is Enfield Cobra Delta, Roger, over"
"Interrogative your latest, over"

We responded by giving our latest position using this code. The major points and rivers are used as landmarks and the code with our location from them would make up the response. In this case the first point, Chon May Point is coded "Any cigarette". Others are "Any Beer", or "Any State", as well as other similar codes. Our response this time was as follows,

"Enfield Cobra Delta, this is Newsboy India XX, our latest Marlboro plus two".
"Newsboy India XX, this is Enfield Cobra Delta, roger your latest, out."

Now that communications have been established, Enfield Cobra Delta begins her transit southward to a meeting point between them and us. We continue to exchange positions until finally the Swift Boat is sighted heading in our direction.

Coming alongside, the OinC's exchange information, the two Vietnamese interpreters exchange information, and the rest of us exchange pleasantries with the other crewmembers. This can take from a few minutes or longer depending on the amount of information passed. With the turnover completed, we move northward to get on station moving at a slower speed to conserve fuel. As soon as we arrive on station, we radio CSC DaNang, call sign "Article". We are now Enfield Cobra Delta and I am on my first full Market Time patrol.

Delta Area was relatively quiet as far as junk traffic goes, mostly sand dunes on the shoreline and one small river. This river was the source of most of the sampan traffic as fishermen came out to cast their nets in the open ocean. There was much larger junk traffic to check since the small boats moved less frequently during the day and not at all during the night. We spent our time running out to seaward, as the large cargo junks would enter our area. The tactic was to approach the cargo junk from the landside and from the rear of the junk. As we moved into range, a button was pressed in the pilothouse causing a loud siren mounted on top of the pilothouse to wail very loud. Usually, the junk would slow its speed and allow us to approach from the stern of the vessel. The Swift would pass alongside the vessel to look it over carefully before coming alongside. Our SVNN interpreter orders the vessel to stop and we come alongside to allow the boarding party to jump aboard. Phoung goes to the steering house to check the vessel's papers while the others of our crew check the cargo hold, the engine room, and the crew areas. Since most of these vessels have the Captain's family on board, there will be cooking areas and sleeping areas to check for contraband. All seems to be in order for this vessel and Mr. Snyder makes a notation in the vessel's papers or "So Ghe". The notation is in English so the vessel's owner cannot read it most of the time however, the note explains the date and time of the search and anything found. A comment about the owner's demeanor or cooperation as we searched his vessel, was entered as well. Then we thanked the vessel owner, gave him a packet of tobacco and papers, wished him well, and gave him some government literature or even a new South Vietnamese flag for his vessel, whatever we had. My skipper brought the Swift Boat alongside to pick us up and we moved away giving the vessel a wave which he returned.

The day moved by quickly and soon RD3 Ken Bloch was cooking dinner in the main cabin. It smelled like fried chicken and I offered to help. Ken thanked me but he was fine in his "kitchen". I climbed down in the engine room to check my oil and water levels before darkness fell and I had to use a red flashlight. Finished with my checks, I checked my oil and water cans for proper tie down, checked my boarding lights and running lights to get ready for nightfall when our patrol tactics would change.

I worked my way down into the main cabin that now had the smell of supper permeating. No C-rations for us, a real cooked meal. Fried chicken prepared in an electric frying pan, vegetables and boiled potatoes make an excellent meal on a 50-foot patrol boat in the South China Sea. We took turns on the watches so everyone could sit down for supper. The sea is calm and the local fishermen are going about their business as we watch the sun set over the mountains to the west. We help Ken Bloch clean up the galley and set the watch for the night. Mr. Snyder is on the radio talking to the troops ashore to see if they would like our mortar services for H & I firing later on tonight. Delta Area does not have any friendly bases on the beach but there are some units operating inland within our mortar range of 2 to 2 ½ miles. Johnnie Fitts sets the watch and the rest of us crawl into the bunks for some sleep. With a curfew in effect, the fishermen must be already anchored before dark and remain so until morning. Anyone traveling after dark is picked up on our radar and demands our immediate attention. So we settle down to a slow patrol speed moving around our area in a random pattern. Landmarks such as a river mouth indicate the patrol areas or a point of land so keeping our position is easy. The watches are pretty simple actually, one man on lookout in the gun tub, another on the radios, with the third man driving and watching the radar. The watches are two hours each and with the stress levels associated with these patrols, it is just right.

The night passes without incident and I find myself on watch as the morning light appears over the ocean. Behind us the fisherman are already moving their sampans and junks out to the fishing grounds they and their ancestors have used for centuries. Most of them do not care who is running the country, communist or South Vietnamese; instead they just want to be left alone in their lives. These are simple people with simple lives and politics is not on their minds at all.

We moved into position near the stream of sampans coming out of the river mouth and hit the siren. Several boats changed course to our position and the first one came alongside. This is our main job, boarding and searching the thousands of junks and sampans that ply the waters of the South China Sea. Quickly, the crew takes positions and prepares to board the first sampan. Phoung is along the starboard side and takes the papers from the fisherman, checking them carefully.

This boarding exercise continues until we hear the welcome radio message that our relief is on the way. We break off from the board and searching and begin to move south

Figure 2. PCF-56 stands by to relieve on station.

to rendezvous with the Swift Boat now transiting to our position. The seas are still calm so we use the time to prepare for entering port, guns cleaned, and engine logs and charts put away.

We headed south and exchange position fixes with the other boat and soon the familiar bow wake of a Swift Boat can be seen heading in our direction. Coming alongside, pubs and intelligence are exchanged. Phoung has some information for the interpreter on the other boat to pass on. Besides, they know each other so I am certain that some personal greetings are exchanged as well. Then it is off to the base in DaNang, a hot shower and a cold beer.

About 1200 we arrive at our berth and move to the pier where we take on ammo and then to the fueling station for diesel fuel. The boat performed well so we don't have any work orders to write for the repair shops. Now all that remains is to clean up the boat and head for the compartment on the APL. This completes my first 24-hour patrol and I am tired and elated to be back at the base. This routine is repeated every other day for the rest of my tour in DaNang and since the newness has not worn off yet, I am still excited to be in the war zone and with a good crew. I am still waiting to get in my first firefight although I feel certain it will be soon.

With the boat rearmed and refueled, the crew heads for the APL and a hot shower. I was getting ready for a shower when my name was announced over the 1MC with instructions to report to the COSDIV12 Office. Wondering what could be up for me, I hurried to the office. Standing there was my brother SPC4 Tom Steffes, US Army. I had last seen Tom in Minnesota while enroute to Swift Boat Training in March and he was on leave having extended for another tour. Tom was stationed in Nha Trang and had wrangled a set of TDY orders to Danang. He was to get a signature from a US Army major in Danang and was allowed two weeks to perform this and visit me as well. We greeted each other warmly and chatted a bit about his mission. I was able to get him a bunk and permission to stay on board the APL during his TDY. I took him over to the wardroom to introduce him to Mr. Snyder. Tom would be allowed to stay with us and go on patrol as a rider. We would be leaving the next morning for a patrol in Area Enfield Cobra Foxtrot Mike, which was the southern most area assigned to CosDiv12 in Danang.

The patrol in Foxtrot Mike area was uneventful, the crew having been there before. It was located off the coast of the Marble Mountain Air Base and had a 3,000 meter restricted zone. This meant that no boat traffic was allowed within this zone and we were kept busy chasing fishing boat traffic out of this area. We found two fishermen with improper papers and took them into custody early in the morning of the second day on patrol. The two fishermen were secured to the lifelines at the stern, given water to drink and brought into Danang when we returned to the base. Our interpreter questioned them but apparently they were not Viet Cong, instead just fishermen with improper papers. They were kept under armed guard just in case after being searched for weapons. We returned to base after being relieved on station and stopped at the Vietnamese Navy Base to drop off our interpreter and the fishermen were turned over to the Vietnamese Authorities. Then it was on to the YR-71 and securing the boat after patrol. Tom had made his first Swift Boat Patrol and returned to base safely.

Our Skipper went to the office and returned with some great news. We were to come off line for a few days and take over our own boat. Another crew led by LTJG Bernard

Wolff had brought PCF-12 from Cam Rahn Bay. This PCF had been overhauled there and was shiny new looking. In order to take over this boat, the crew had to inspect and inventory all the equipment prior to signing the documents relating to the boat. I loaned my brother some dungarees so he wouldn't get his greens all greasy and together we climbed into the engine room and other spaces to complete the inspections. We spent this time enjoying each other's company and getting this job done. By the time we finished, Tom felt more like a sailor than a soldier for a while. With the turnover complete, PCF-12 went on its first patrol with its new crew. The area was Enfield Cobra Foxtrot, which is south of Monkey Mountain and off the coast of the Danang Air Base and China Beach R & R Center. We beached the boat on a soft sandy beach behind Monkey Mountain and finished cleaning the sides and checking the screws and rudders in the clear water. Mr. Snyder ordered swim call and we all enjoyed the break and the warm water of the South China Sea. It was a routine patrol and we returned the next day full of confidence in our new boat. PCF-12 was ours and as we made the turn around Monkey Mountain, I pushed the throttles forward, feeling the surge of power from her twin Detroit Diesels. It felt really well having our own boat. As we became one with crew and boat, I believed that if we took care of her, she would take care of us. Returning to base with a new sense of pride, our after patrol checks took on new meanings as we refueled and then tied up PCF-12 alongside her sisters at the YR-71.

The date was June 14th and it was time for Tom to return to his base in Nha Trang. We would be leaving the next day for Enfield Cobra Charlie, the second area below the DMZ and the farthest north patrol for me. Tom and I went to the EM Club in Camp Tien Sha for a final drink together, reflecting on these last few days. He was back in his greens and we had taken some pictures aboard PCF-12 together. The next morning Tom took a picture of our crew together and several of the boat as PCF-12 left the APL heading out to sea.

The only other exercise that we went through as a division occurred when the enemy would fire rockets into to the Air Base, which happened at least once while I was there. All of the boats in port are manned and scrambled to specific positions throughout the harbor area. The patrol roster for the day gave each crew their assignments in the event of this scramble. It did not seem like a war zone so far except for the constant rumble of jets taking off from the air base and the constant star shell flares hanging in the night sky near the base perimeters.

I did not know it at the time but my crew and I were headed for a moment in history that would change our lives forever. I would meet people in later years that shared this moment as well. In the next chapter, I will identify these units and the people stationed there that I would meet in my research and become close friends with many of them.

CHAPTER SIX

Allied Units in the Area and Their Locations

I n this chapter, I will identify these Allied Units and the personnel within them whom I met many years later during my investigations of this incident. At the time of the incident, I did not know many of these people or their units by name.

Figure 3. A South Vietnamese Navy Yabuta Junk assigned to a Coastal Group

Besides the Coastal Surveillance Centers, or CSC, there are other units of Market Time that Swift Boats would come in contact on a daily basis. Among these are the Coastal Groups located along the coastline of South Vietnam. They consist of a small group of Naval Advisors to a contingent of South Vietnamese Navy Yabuta Junk Boats. These boats were wooden and lightly armed with only a 30 Caliber machine gun or two and small arms. They conduct board and search operations among the fisherman and other water traffic similar to the Swift Boats and Coast Guard Craft.

In the I Corps Area, there was one Coastal Group in Cua Viet; one in Tan My, which is inside the entrance to the Perfume River; one south of Diem Truong which leads to a large inland lake populated by many villages and hamlets; one inside DaNang harbor near the Swift Base; and one at the entrance to the Cua Dai River south of DaNang, which is the southern tip of Coastal Division Twelve Operations Area. To the south of the Cua Dai River is another Operations Area patrolled by units out of Chu Lai, which is a detachment of Coastal Division Twelve. Coastal Groups were strategically located along the coastline all the way to the Cambodian Border. Swift Boats on patrol worked closely with these Coastal Groups to share intelligence and to ensure that our gunfire missions did not cause problems with friendly South Vietnamese villages.

These Coastal Group Advisors came under Commander Task Force 115, Market Time, commanded by Captain Roy F. Hoffmann based at Cam Rahn Bay.

Figure 4. Coastal Group 14 with PCF-12 moored at the pier.

The Northernmost Patrol Area was known as Enfield Cobra Alpha and extended from the Demilitarized Zone, or DMZ, south to several miles below Cua Viet. This area was about 100 miles north of our Swift Base in DaNang and required several hours of transit time even in good weather conditions. In order to shorten this transit time and the period in which a Swift Boat did not man the area, different options were tried to solve this problem. One was to station several Swift Boats and crews in Cua Viet Harbor. However, a lack of available repair facilities, the extremely rough water in the channel entrance during acclimate weather, and the constant shelling of the area by North Vietnamese Artillery posed problems more severe than the transit time. Cua Viet was a forward supply base for supporting the U.S. Marines based along the southern edge of the DMZ. Supplies, such as ammunition, food, and spare parts for the Marines and their vehicles moved steadily northward from DaNang by Yard Freight Utility, or YFU, and Landing Craft Utility, or LCU's. These boats were a constant target of these North Vietnamese Gunners as they transited the Cua Viet River and made stops at the piers in Cua Viet. During rough weather and especially during the Northern Monsoon Period, the channel into Cua Viet was almost impossible to transit. High waves and swells would toss smaller lighter craft, such as a Swift Boat, back and forth while pushing them toward the entrance similar to a surf board on the crest of a wave. On at least one occasion, a Swift Boat capsized and nearly swamped another trying to rescue the crew. At least one sailor was lost in this tragedy. Lack of spare parts and repair facilities for the Swift Boats was accomplished by sending a few repair personnel from DaNang to assist the boat crews, however, a major casualty such as an engine or hull damage required a trip to DaNang. This plan was abandoned after a short period of time.

Figure 5. A U.S. Coast Guard WHEC with a Swift Boat alongside.

The next option, and the one in place at the time of the incident, was to station two crews and one Swift Boat aboard a Coast Guard Vessel, such as a WHEC, or High Endurance Cutter; or a U.S. Navy DER, or Destroyer Escort. These units were already assigned to Market Time and provided berthing, fuel, ammunition, and a limited repair source for the Swift Boats.

Since these units were already at sea, the transiting of the Cua Viet Channel was avoided and with the mother ship turned to give a shelter in its lee, a Swift Boat could

Figure 6. PCF-19 came alongside USS Boston to deliver passengers.

come alongside and receive services, change crews, or even just to take shelter during a storm without compromising the mission of this critical patrol area.

At this time the mother ship on station near the DMZ was USCG Campbell WHEC-32, commanded by Captain R.B. Long Jr. On June 10th, 1968, PCF-19 commanded by LTJG Doug Burgess, departed DaNang for the DMZ area with the crew of LTJG John Davis on board. After a long transit up the coast, PCF-19 arrived alongside Campbell, which would be their temporary home for two weeks. John Davis and his crew climbed aboard with their gear and went below to their quarters. Some of the personal gear of Ltjg Burgess' crew was also brought aboard to clear the PCF of excess gear that could get in the way during patrol. With handshakes all around, the crew of Campbell welcomed the Swift Boat sailors to this world of Coast Guard shipboard life. It was not too much of a culture shock however because sailors are sailors and Coast Guard shipboard routine in the war zone was not much different than their U.S. Navy counterparts. As they moved below, they looked back; PCF-19 was moving off to toward the South Vietnamese coastline, taking station as Enfield Cobra Alpha. Later, she would hook up with another U.S. Coast Guard vessel, U.S.C.G. Cutter Point Dume (WPB-82325), commanded by LTJG Ronald E. Fritz. Point Dume was on station at this time as Enfield Cobra Victor Alpha and due to her size and other mission capabilities, made her invaluable in maintaining a presence at the DMZ area. Her mission was to track and interdict boat traffic near the coastline and to board and search the larger vessels moving along the coast in the two to five mile distance from the shore. Working with the PCF on station, this team formed a barrier to the enemy's efforts to move supplies and material into the south. She could also remain on station during the periods of PCF's transiting from their home base and extreme rough weather that kept the smaller PCF's in port. This cutter would also receive much of its fuel and ammunition and other supplies by entering Cua Viet and returning to station. The Coast Guard Ships offshore were also able to provide parts and material to the Point Dume when the Cua Viet River entrance was impassable due to bad weather.

Farther out to sea along the coastline were U.S. Navy Ships that were assigned to Operation Market Time and others were part of Sea Dragon Operations. These ships moved in and out of these areas to provide Naval Gunfire Support for Allied Forces ashore and to stop and board the large oceangoing vessels moving through the area. They would move out to sea to replenish stores and take on fuel and ammunition. This meant that ships could be off DaNang for several days and be at the DMZ or farther north for up to a week or so at a time. These movements were coordinated by Group Commanders and when attached to Market Time, Commander TF-115 in Cam Rahn Bay. This Commander at this time was Captain Roy F. Hoffmann.

Among the ships in this group that are mentioned because they were involved in the PCF-19 incident are the following; USS Boyd DD-544, my contact is a Radarman named Mike Stowe who was a forward lookout on the night of the incident; USS Edson DD-946; USS Boston CAG-1, commanded by Captain Leon I. Smith. A young Ensign on board during this time by the name of John Taylor is my contact; USS Theodore E. Chandler DD-717 with DESRON 9 on board, my contact is a RD3 by the name of Jim Fitch; USS Blandy DD-943, USS Sanctuary AH-17, USS Repose AH-16, and USS Acme MSO-508, commanded by LCDR M.K. Overholser, my contacts include HM1 Larry Lail, a Boatswains Mate named Dave Campbell, and an Engineman named Tom Doble. One other Allied Ship was part of this group and the target of friendly fire resulting in casualties was HMAS Hobart D-39. The above named ships will be discussed further concerning their involvement in later chapters. Some were together at the same time and others were operating independently of each other when the incident occurred.

There were land-based units that were involved in this incident and their identification follows. They were U.S. Marines stationed at small outposts scattered along the Southern Edge of the Demilitarized Zone. Some of these outposts made up the MacNamara Line, a series of bases connected to stop the interdiction of troops and supplies across the DMZ. These units were part of the 3rd Marine Division headquartered in DaNang. Specific units of the 3rd Marine Division were involved in the sighting and later witnesses to the sinking of PCF-19. These included the 1st Amphibian Tractor Battalion, commanded by LtCol G.F. Meyers and based at the Cua Viet Port Facility, Republic of Vietnam. Within this battalion were Company "A", commanded by Major R.B. Throm; Company "B", commanded by Major J.C. Burger Jr., "S-3", commanded by Major D.R. Stefansson and one of the radio operators, Cpl John "Andy" Anderson, who worked with all three of these elements when they were in these forward positions.

There were also several NGLO, or Naval Gunfire Liaison Officers assigned to American and South Vietnamese units to coordinate Naval Gunfire in support of military operations along the DMZ. My contact is Ltjg Pete Sullivan.

The U.S. Air Force was involved as well. The 480th Tactical Fighter Squadron, called "Gunfighters", commanded by Colonel Don Damico. It was based in DaNang Air Base flying F-4 Phantoms.

Each of these units cited in this chapter have one or more witnesses to this incident and will be reflected in later chapters. All have made statements to me as to their involvement and the facts of the incident they witnessed. These witnesses vary in capacity from a forward bridge lookout to the watch officer in Combat Information Center on a cruiser. Others were Air Force Pilots down to radio operators in field combat units. All saw the same aircraft flying over the DMZ and many years later came together to tell the same story as the other witnesses. It was an event that bonded them together and remained in memory all these years just as clear as if it had just happened.

CHAPTER SEVEN

Moving Toward a Moment in History

In the period of late May and into June of 1968, there were many battles, contact with the enemy forces, and attacks on our bases and ships. There were also some larger "Search and Destroy" missions being conducted in the northern areas. Some of these missions required participation and or coordination between Allied Units of the same command or even different branches of the military forces. Ground units were using Air Force, Marine and Navy Aircraft, Naval Guns offshore, and ground artillery from firebases, to prep the battlefield and soften up the enemy forces as they moved forward into battle. These operations required communications between units and forces to accomplish their mission as well as to prevent accidental attacks on friendly forces. These accidental attacks did take place all too frequently in the fog of war and only careful planning can reduce these casualties. One of the famous ones involved an attack in 1965 on a USCG WPB 82ft Cutter off the DMZ. U.S. Air Force Jet Planes attacked the Point Welcome repeatedly even though the cutter used flashing lights, flags and many other types of communications, they failed to ward off the repeated attacks on this vessel. One of the results of this incident's investigation was the painting of a white star on a blue circle atop the pilothouse of all U.S. Small Craft plying the waters of South Vietnam. Even so, one had to feel a little nervous when several friendly jets or helicopters flew over our boats at low altitudes. Since Swift Boats ventured above the DMZ during the course of our patrols, we checked in with the Marine shore units along the DMZ and gave them our intentions and timetable. The Swift Boats would go up mostly at night and using the NOD, or night observation device, (starlight scope for short) watch for the enemy trying to slip into the south aboard small sampans or fishing junks. Disguised as innocent fishermen, they would use the cover of darkness or the background of the coastline to move along the coast.

It was under this atmosphere that the incident of PCF-19 occurred. U.S. Marine units along the DMZ, as well as Swift Boat and Coast Guard Crews sighted and reported single and multiple groups of lights moving between the coastline and the offshore island named "Tiger Island". Tiger Island was long suspected of being supplied from the mainland in some way because large shore batteries had been installed and the North Vietnamese had used them to attack our destroyers and cruisers as they maneuvered in this DMZ area of operations. The Tiger Island forces were also used to report movements of our ships enabling the larger shore guns on the mainland to attack our ships as well.

These "lights" were only seen at night and were red and green with blinking lights on these aircraft. They were called "UFO's" by our forces because they were unidentified. These "aircraft" had the ability to hover and move at slow or fast speeds at various altitudes. Although they did not normally show to be offensive in nature, they did fly dangerously close to Allied Units on patrol to the south of the Ben Hai River. My sources found that these reports of UFO's were usually downplayed at the highest level for some reason but whatever they were, the lights moved back and forth every night. With many nightly patrols and troop movement along the DMZ, it was unknown whether these UFO's were tracking these patrols or just going about their business on the North Vietnamese side of the DMZ.

In the early part of June, the Marines conducted numerous operations in their area of operations resulting in clashes with North Vietnamese forces and continual shelling from the North Vietnamese Batteries to the north. Day to day operations in Cua Viet would be interrupted by several rounds of "incoming" artillery aimed at ammo dumps, fuel storage and the many LCU/YFU craft carrying supplies up the Cua Viet River. In the early part of June, Company B, 1st Amtrac Battalion was at Base Area C-4. Commanded by Major Burger, this unit conducted operations along the beach line and a short distance inland. CPL John "Andy" Anderson was the radio operator with this unit and detailed to me the close coordination by radio between the Swift Boat Units operating offshore and his unit. This communication was vital in getting some close mortar support from the PCF's on a number of occasions. When the Swift Boats sighted the UFO's, the sightings were verified by radio with Andy and other units along the DMZ. Another base nearby was Oceanview manned by elements of "B" Company, 1st Amtrac Battalion, 3rd Marines and they were the first to "officially" report UFO's. Their report in the monthly summary stated, "UFO's in vicinity YD 2674, YD 2582, and YD 2583, reported by Blurry Critic "L". All Towers were alerted; UFO's appear to be helicopters. Notified CO and put Battalion on blackout status." This was on June 15th, in the evening, time unknown.

On the morning of June 15th, Swift Boats from DaNang departed the base at various times to rendezvous and relieve all the patrol areas except Enfield Cobra Alpha. Alpha was manned by PCF-19 with the crew of Ltjg Doug Burgess on board. As daybreak brightened to early morning, PCF-19 headed seaward to rendezvous with USCG Campbell to rearm, refuel and change crews. As reported by the Swift Boat crews, the UFO's were up and flying the night before just as they had been most nights before, however, they had not made any threatening gestures or even seemed to know the Swift Boats were there. Rearmed, refueled, and ready to proceed, Ltjg John Davis and his crew departed the side of USCG Campbell and moved into the patrol area.

The USS Boston CAG-1 was operating about 13 miles off the DMZ. USS Chandler DD-717 steamed in company with USS Blandy DD-943. USS Edson DD-946 and HMAS Hobart D-39, were operating near Dong Hoi east of Cap Lay. Cap Lay is a mountainous cape about 10 miles north of the DMZ and directly westward of Tiger Island. These ships were conducting harassment and interdiction fire at targets inside North Vietnam. USS Boston had an antiquated fire control system and Terrier Surface to air missiles, relying on her 8-inch guns to fire at the enemy. Few if any North Vietnamese aircraft dared to venture this far south or to try to penetrate the air defense systems of the Allied Ships. USS Boyd DD544 an older destroyer was operating independently near the DMZ. USS Acme MSO-508 was operating in Market Time near DaNang. The Hospital Ships USS Repose and USS Sanctuary were operating between Hue and Cua Viet from 8 to 10 miles offshore. Working with these ships and the shore-based forces was the Fire Raider Naval Gunfire Spotter Team with Ltjg Pete Sullivan. He was positioned at Oceanview.

Further south, PCF-69, commanded by Ltjg Bernard Wolff was moving into position as Enfield Cobra Charlie Mike, just north of Hue. PCF-12, commanded by Ltjg Pete Snyder, moved into position off Wonder Beach south of Cua Viet as Enfield Cobra Charlie. The crew of PCF-12 consisted of BM2 Johnnie P. Fitts, GMGSN Tom Klemash, RD3 Ken Bloch, QM3 Gary Rosenberger, EN2 James Steffes and Phuong our Vietnamese interpreter. It was a bright sunny day, the seas were relatively calm, boat traffic in our area was light, allowing us to move to seaward to search some larger cargo junks moving through our area. USCG Point Dume was on station as Enfield Cobra Victor Alpha. Each of us doing our assigned job in a war that seemed to be all around us yet did not always involve us. That would all change later that evening as all these units became involved in a deadly incident.

CHAPTER EIGHT

Action in the Demilitarized Zone

P CF-12 boarded and searched several cargo junks headed for Hue to load cargo and one large fishing junk operating out of Danang.

Figure 7. PCF-12 prepares to board a Vietnamese steel hull.

He seemed a long way from home but his papers were in order so he was allowed to continue on his way. An American Navy gasoline tanker moved into our area and tied up to a buoy off the Wonder Beach causeway. A fuel hose connected to the buoy reached ashore to a fuel storage area. The tanker brought fuel for the Huey helicopters belonging to the Army's 1st Cavalry Division based at Wonder Beach. Several LCU's or Landing Craft Utility transited the area heavily loaded with supplies bound for Cua Viet and the U.S. Marines operating there.

The crew of PCF-12 settled down to a dinner of pork chops and fried potatoes prepared by RD3 Ken Bloch. The patrol seemed routine so far and after dinner we all prepared our equipment and spaces for night operations.

A radio call from Enfield Cobra Alpha asking for help brought me to the pilothouse. PCF-19 was having trouble with her radar, at slow speed the display would grow faint and she was unable to verify her position accurately. It sounded to me as if the starboard engine was not charging the batteries properly. PCF-19 asked if they could rendezvous with us for assistance. Mr. Snyder coded up our position and a rendezvous point was agreed upon. Both Swift Boats moved toward this position at maximum speed in order to check out the problem before darkness fell. I learned that PCF-19 although similar to PCF-12 had some differences in the battery circuits. PCF-12 had a switch on the after bulkhead that enabled the two battery banks to be connected together. PCF-19 did not have this switch and the crew did not know if there were jumper cables on board. I did have a spare set and decided to use them to connect the battery banks together thus enabling PCF-19's port engine to charge both battery banks. We prepared flashlights and my cables for PCF-19's arrival.

Dusk was rapidly closing in when we spotted the bow wake of Enfield Cobra Alpha. Soon she was tied up alongside and I jumped aboard with the cables. I did not know the crew of LTJG John Davis but the rest of my crew did, having been in country longer than I. I was introduced to EN2 Ed Cruz, the engineer on his crew. Ed was from Guam and greeted me warmly as I stepped aboard PCF-19. PCF-19 had been at sea continuously since leaving Danang on June 10th. changing crews every 24 hours. He explained to me that his problem was keeping the radar operational which became more difficult as the patrol moved into the darkness of the night. Board and Search Lights, radios, and running lights were weak and dim due to the starboard battery bank condition. He had checked the water levels and they were full and the connections were tight and free of corrosion. This led us to believe the alternator on the starboard engine was not charging properly. Together, we checked the connections in the charging circuit and the belt tension on the alternator. There did not appear to be any problems there either and we did not have a voltmeter to check output of the charging circuit. I suggested to him that we use my jumper cables to connect the two battery banks together thus enabling the port engine's charging system to charge both banks at the same time. Since Swift Boat electrical systems routed most of the major equipment to specific battery banks, it was impossible to rewire these circuits in the dark while underway. So there we were, my new found friend and I, hooking up these homemade jumper cables, using a red flashlight and getting small shocks as we hooked them up, laughing together and then cheering as the crew called down to tell us the running lights were coming on bright again. Mission accomplished, we climbed out of the engine room and checked the radar and the board and search lights for signs that the jumper cables and the port engine were doing their job. Heading back up north at high speed should put some juice back in the batteries for sure. As we wiped the grease from our hands and dungarees, Ed Cruz and

I talked about how our respective boats were running and I asked him if he needed any extra rags, oil or water, or anything else I had to spare. His boat was very close to mine in design being PCF-12 and 19.

While we were busy in the engine room, the rest of the crew exchanged information with each other and we learned that LTJG Davis had wanted to bring his boat, PCF-80, on this mission but Ltjg Burgess insisted on bringing his boat PCF-19. PCF-80 had just completed an upkeep period on the skids in Danang and the crew wished they could have brought it instead. Having your own boat on patrol is much easier since you maintain it and have your own tools, parts, and extra supplies as well as knowing the little quirks that every boat has.

With everything running smoothly again we said goodbye to PCF-19 and she moved away, swinging her bows northward, returning to her patrol area. A short burst of her siren as she sped away while we waved to our friends not knowing we would never see some of them again.

It was nearing 2100 hours and our crew returned to the routine of night patrol. The first watch was set and the rest of us lay down for a couple hours sleep. For me, sleep did not come easy as I thought about our "quick fix" and whether PCF-19 would be able to make more permanent repairs on board Campbell. More than likely she would have to return to Danang unless an alternator could be found in Cua Viet. I said a little prayer of thanks for PCF-12, which was running good and dozed off to sleep.

At 2330, I was awakened to relieve the watch by 2345 and I dressed quickly because I wanted to hear if there was any news from PCF-19. LTJG Snyder informed us that he had just spoken with LTJG Davis and his boat and the radar were doing fine. He did not give his location at that time. I assumed the watch on the helm under a mostly cloudy sky with a bright moon that appeared briefly through the clouds. The seas were calm and a gently rolling swell made for easy sleeping as PCF-12 moved north just a few miles off the shore. I checked the radar and it was clear, most of the boat traffic was either in their villages or farther out to sea. BM2 Fitts was at the chart table and GMG3 Kelmash was on lookout in the forward gun tub. This quiet patrol would be interrupted by the radio crackling to life. At approximately 0030, a "Flash Traffic" message to all Market Time Units, message to follow, blared from the speaker. I grabbed my pen and the logbook and began to copy a message in code. BM2 Fitts went down to wake Mr. Snyder as I opened the codebooks to decode the message. It was from the observers at Alpha One, located on the southern edge of the DMZ. It stated that they had been tracking Enfield Cobra Alpha near the Ben Hai River and she had disappeared in a flash of light. They feared that she had been sunk. Mr. Snyder entered the pilothouse and read the message quickly. He took over the watch and contacted Alpha One and USCG Point Dume asking if assistance was needed. Point Dume replied that she was on the site and searching for survivors and would like assistance. I woke the rest of the crew and PCF-12 headed northward at max speed. A message to Article in Danang informing them of our intention was quickly written up and sent by Mr. Snyder. My thoughts were racing as I wondered what could have happened to PCF-19 and my new friends. I went below to the engine room and switched to my other fuel tanks while I had the time to spare. BM2 Fitts found me on the stern and we proceeded to open up the 81MM illumination rounds from their cardboard containers. Meanwhile, the rest of the crew made preparations to render assistance when we arrived. This is not something one trains for but our instincts took over and all of us moved as one team. Medical kits were taken out, extra ammunition was passed up to the gunner in the gun tub, and flak jackets and life jackets were laid out in the main cabin.

Unknown to us at the time, Article sent a message to all Market Time Units to move up one patrol area to fill the gap created when we left our patrol area. Ltjg Wolfe in PCF-69 moved from Enfield Cobra Charlie Mike to Charlie and so forth down to line. We received a message ordering us to assume Enfield Cobra Alpha.

The adrenalin was pumping as were arrived at the location of the sinking. There were small amounts of debris and a large fuel and oil slick on the surface. Point Dume was on the scene and was lifting one of the survivors from the water. PCF-12 moved alongside and voices carried across the decks as Mr. Snyder was briefed on the situation so far. Point Dume crewman rescued the skipper LTJG John Davis, and one crewman from the water. Both were badly wounded and in need of immediate evacuation to a hospital. Point Dume headed for Cua Viet and we took up the search. There was a current moving north along the coast at this point so we had to work quickly to locate any more survivors. The 81MM mortar was uncovered and as I loaded the illumination round into the tube, BM2 Fitts, the gunner fired them into the sky. They burst into a bright light that floated down on a parachute. All eyes were on the surface of the water as round after round was fired into the air. Moving the boat around we searched until I informed Mr. Snyder that we had only one round left. It was fired into the sky and we searched in vain until the round burned out and dropped into the sea. Suddenly there were four more illumination rounds popping into view over our heads. They were slightly amber in color not bright white as ours were. Mr. Snyder came back to ask where these rounds came from? We told him we did not know and we were out of illumination. They were not ours. With Point Dume still in Cua Viet and no one else around us, he concluded that they belonged to the enemy since we were very close if not inside North Vietnamese waters. PCF-12 leaped to full speed and left the search area heading southward. The illumination rounds continued to light our track as new ones replaced those dropping into the sea. We were followed for some distance by these illumination shells. At some point they stopped and darkness returned around us. At this time PCF12 slowed to a stop. Checking the radar to make certain of our position, Mr. Snyder called on the radio for assistance in what to do with this new development. Were the illumination rounds from our ships off shore or the Marines inland? Were they trying to help us locate survivors by lighting up the sky for us? None of the ships or shore units on our frequency responded that it was them. I did not notice any aircraft lights around us during this time but we were pretty busy and the crew did not indicate later that any aircraft were around us. PCF-12 was now off the entrance to Cua Viet about three miles out to sea as near as we could spot our position. Suddenly, two sets of aircraft lights appeared off our port and starboard beam, about 300 yards away and 100 feet above the water. They just sat there not moving and we were sitting still in the water as well. I raced up to the pilothouse and tapped Mr. Snyder on the shoulder, pointing at the lights. QM3 Gary Rosenberger was on the helm and he turned the boat to face one of the aircraft thus giving a low profile to the two aircraft and allowing the guns to bear in case they appeared to be threatening. Since they did not fly over us at this point we believed they were helicopters. The question was; were they ours or were they unfriendly? Mr. Snyder began calling on the radios for assistance in identifying these two helos that just hovered off our position not moving. The observers at Alpha One and Ocean View reported that they were indeed not moving and were of unknown origin. As radio traffic crackled back and forth, the shore units attempted to find out whether the U.S. Army or any of the ships offshore had any helos in the air. The Forward Air Controllers or NGLOS reported that these aircraft were not "squawking IFF". IFF is a transponder used on allied aircraft to identify themselves as "friendly aircraft". It shows up on radar sometimes as a "blinking dot" and sometimes as the identification of the aircraft and call sign depending on the type of radar.

About fifteen minutes had passed by now and the aircraft were still there although it seemed like hours since they were first spotted. Mr. Snyder requested to take them under fire repeatedly and repeatedly received the response from Article to "wait one". We heard radio traffic from "Latch" Captain Roy F. Hoffmann trying to reach us but although we could hear him, he could not hear us. It is several hundred miles from our position to where he was in Cam Rahn Bay. He was Commander Task Force 115 known as Market Time. Article could hear him and us so they began to relay traffic between Latch and us. This slowed things down somewhat but at least communication was established between our "big boss" and this tiny gunboat facing down two unidentified helicopters on the edge of the border between North and South Vietnam. Mr. Snyder decided to move us more to the south in case we were attacked our position would be well inside South Vietnamese waters.

As PCF-12 moved slowly southward, the moon came out from behind a cloud and I observed the helo facing us as we moved toward it and then turned away. I saw a round clear nose with what appeared to be two men sitting side by side in the aircraft. A red light under the aircraft was blinking and other lights were steady red and green. I walked along the deck to the pilothouse and told Mr. Snyder that I got a good look at the aircraft and it appeared to remain stationary as we passed. Mr. Snyder call up to GMGSN Klemash to come down and take the helm so QM3 Rosenberger could assist RD3 Bloch with the radios. He was sitting on the edge of the gun tub when he saw the helo to starboard fire the rocket.I walked back to the stern and as I passed the after controls position, I felt a rush of heat and the hair on my neck stood up. I turned my head to see a small explosion in the water off our port beam. Apparently, the other aircraft fired a rocket that passed between our antennas and exploded in the water. Mr. Snyder must have heard it as well as PCF-12 jumped to max speed to clear the area. We drove at this speed making zigzag patterns so as not to be a clear target. GMGSN Klemash and BM2 Fitts opened up with all guns as the Swift Boat moved quickly from the kill zone. GMGSN Klemash kept firing his 50's at the blinking lights until he heard a sound of glass breaking and the light went out. After a short time we stopped again to look around. At first there was nothing to see but then the two aircraft appeared off our beams again with lights on. They would move around as we turned keeping their distance, turning their lights on and sometimes off as they kept their positions. Mr. Snyder again asked the NGLO ashore if these aircraft were in sight to them. They replied "Yes, we have you and two aircraft on radar and starlight scope." "Are they squawking IFF? He asked. "Negative, I repeat negative squawking IFF," came the reply.

My OinC said, "Roger that, I am taking UFO's under fire if they show hostile intent".

It was not clear if these two aircraft were the same ones that attacked us a few minutes earlier. By this time, the helicopters were forward and aft of our position and I observed the forward helo open fire with a single machine gun located in its nose. Our guns returned fire and GMGSN Tom Klemash hammered away with the twin 50's on the forward helo and BM2 Johnnie Fitts with the after 50 caliber at the other one until they broke contact and left the area with their lights out. For the next two to two and one half hours, we played cat and mouse with one or more helos at a time using the same tactics however they seemed to keep their distance and would move away when we opened fire. GMGSN Klemash advised Mr. Snyder that his ammo was getting low and the reply was to use it sparingly. I moved back and forth carrying ammunition to both gunners and had a hard time keeping up. During this time I heard the radio calls and listened to Mr. Snyder directing the fire and issuing orders. At one point I observed Point Dume firing tracers up into the air but was unable to see any lights near her from this distance. During this time the radios were crackling constantly as my OinC answered calls and talked to Danang as all friendly aircraft that could be in the area were checked out. The result was: No friendlies lost or operating in the area, these had to be North Vietnamese.

About 0330, low on ammunition and barrels burned out in the machine guns, PCF-12 received a call from an aircraft flight leader as they approached from the south to intercept. PCF-12 and Point Dume were to fire a blue flare to identify our positions. The jets flew overhead and acknowledged our positions. There were explosions and blinking lights to the north as the jets looked for targets. Remember, this is at least three hours after PCF-19 was sunk.

As dawn broke over the sea, PCF-12 went alongside a destroyer and received fuel and ammunition. It had been a long night and as we moved over the position where PCF-19 had sunk, the oil and debris had already begun to disperse.

Later on that morning, PCF-12 was relieved by PCF-101 and we returned to base in Danang. Mr. Snyder would write an after action report and Point Dume would return to base and do the same. The next day, the 17th, I believe, both crews and some other witnesses were called to III Marine Air Force Headquarters where a Board of Inquiry was begun. The war continued up north but for now PCF-12's crew was involved in the inquiry.

At the inquiry, I was called in to testify and was asked to describe the helicopter that I saw and an artist drew a picture based on my description. The helicopter that I described to the artist was a Russian Built MI4 "Hound" helicopter. Gary Rosenberger was also testifying that he saw a fixed wing aircraft fly over us without lights. Several members of Point Dume's crew testified as well.

As for me, I do not remember hearing the results of the inquiry, not even through the "grapevine". Our crew went to the DMZ in August with another crew for two weeks using USCG Owasco as a mother ship. Thoughts of that night faded with the tempo of patrols and later PCF-12 moved to Chu Lai where I remained until after January 1st of 1969. It was at a Christmas Party for CosDiv12 in December 1968 that I learned the findings of the Informal Board of Inquiry which I appeared before, as well as the more Formal Board that convened in July 1968 in Hawaii. The Official Findings were "Friendly Fire" and because there were pieces of an American Missile found on Boston and Hobart, the Air Force was blamed for the attack. I was transferred with another crew to Coastal Division Thirteen in Cat Lo near the Mekong Delta. I would finish my tour on Swift Boats patrolling the Co Chein and Ham Lhong Rivers and making raids as part of Operation Sea Lords. I returned to the U.S. in June 1969. I made a career of the Navy and retired in 1985. I did not think much about these events but when I did, they haunted me because the official decision was that these men were killed by "friendly fire". The news accounts had said that missiles from American Jets hit the HMAS Hobart and USS Boston and that these same jets were responsible for sinking a Navy Patrol Boat the same night. What did not make sense was that missiles hit Hobart and Boston on June 17th and PCF-19 and us were attacked on June 16th. Since I did not meet any other Swifty during the rest of my career, I had no way of knowing what really happened. Could it be that there were some political motives for the "official decision" of friendly fire? Time would tell as the years rolled by with these questions nagging at me at various times in my life. I did not know then but there were others who were there that night that felt the same about the incident as I did. Thanks to the innovation of the Internet and other events that took place, many of us would find each other and work to resolve this issue.

CHAPTER NINE

The 1990's Bring News and Old Friends to Light

In the early days of 1995, I was living in San Diego and I answered an ad in a VFW Magazine for a proposed reunion of Swift Boat Sailors to be held in Phoenix, Arizona over Memorial Day, 1995. It seems a retired Hospital Corpsman named Joseph Quartuccio, living in Sierra Vista, Arizona, had served with Swift Boats in both Danang and An Thoi in the early years of 1965 and 1966. He would read the reunions column in the VFW magazine every month and wonder why such a group of veterans never had a reunion. One day, he decided to run an ad and see what response he could get. He decided on Memorial Day weekend in Phoenix and before long he had almost twenty guys committed to this gathering.

It was very informal and some of the guys brought their wives as well. For three days we talked, drank beer and remembered old friends and wondered where they all were. One of those men attending was Jim Thomas who was part of a larger effort to gather these veterans unbeknown to us in Arizona. He had been part of the Game Wardens of Vietnam and had attended a reunion in Las Vegas, Nevada the previous year. Several Swifties were in attendance as well and for various reasons, they decided to embark on a mission to form an organization of Swift Boat Sailors and their support personnel. As they gathered names from the Mobile Riverine Force Assn, another Brown Water Veterans Group, they found another group involved in bringing back two Swift Boats from Panama. The two boats would be restored and dedicated in June 1995 just a few weeks after the Swifties gathered in Arizona. Jim Thomas brought to us a proposal for a Swift Boat Organization along with a set of bylaws and constitution. The eighteen of us in Phoenix signed these first articles which were presented to a larger group at the dedication of the two Swift Boats in Washington D.C, in June 1995. The result was that the Swift Boat Sailors Association was formed. The mission of this group was to seek out other Swifties, as we were called, and to gather every other year for fellowship and to remember our fallen comrades. Among the first members of the new organization was Admiral Elmo Zumwalt Jr. who had been COMMANDER NAVAL FORCES VIETNAM from September 1968 to September 1969 and the father of the Sea Lords Operations. He was our "big boss" in country and held a special place in his heart for the Brown Water Navy, and Swift Boats were a very large part of it.

It was at the gathering in Phoenix that my life changed in a very big way. It happened one morning as we were having breakfast in the hotel patio and I sat down next to Doc Quartuccio. He was talking to Jim Thomas about a letter he had received asking for information on PCF-19 in 1968. He wanted him to ask around in Washington D.C. at the dedication of PCF-1 and 2 for someone that could help this person. My ears perked up and I asked if I could help. This letter was from a retired Chief Hospital Corpsman named Larry Lail from Charlotte Court House, Virginia. It contained a phone number and his address. I agreed to contact him when I returned to California.

When I called Larry a few days later, he was ecstatic to hear from someone so soon. I explained who I was and that I had been on PCF-12 that night in June 1968. He was the corpsman aboard USS Acme (MSO-508) and they were on Market Time Station near Danang when they received a message to proceed to the Cua Viet area near the DMZ. They arrived early morning on June 16th and were met by PCF-101 carrying four divers. Using their sonar, Acme was to locate the sunken wreck of a Navy Swift Boat hit by enemy fire about eight hours earlier. Their mission was to support the divers as they removed the bodies, weapons, and equipment from the wreck. The divers would then destroy the boat using explosives to deny the enemy any use of the equipment on board. Larry had received four bodies as they were brought aboard over the next three days and processed the paperwork required in these cases. He had been a Fleet Marine Force Corpsman on a previous tour so was very familiar with handling remains especially those torn apart by enemy weapons. He remembers retrieving four bodies, two Caucasian and two appearing to be oriental or Asian. One was dressed in South Vietnamese Navy uniform and carried two sets of Vietnamese papers. The others had no identification on them however one of the Caucasian bodies had a tattoo of a deer's head on his arm. One body was delivered to USS Sanctuary (AH-17) on June 16th and the other two delivered to the Hospital in Danang. The South Vietnamese Sailor was turned over to the Vietnamese Navy in Danang. He recalls there being a large Naval presence in the area with a lot of aircraft flying around during the search and recovery mission. When they were finished, Acme resumed her Market Time mission and Larry went on with his life. However, he always wondered and had many nightmares about that mission and those torn bodies he placed in body bags and delivered to Danang. He thought about their names, which he did not know, their families, their hometowns, and what this tragedy meant to all of them. He wished he could find them and let them know that he had handled the remains of their sons and husbands aboard PCF-19 with dignity and respect. It was during one of his periods of reflection on this event when he saw the ad in the VFW magazine for Doc Quartuccio's gathering of Swift Boat Sailors in Phoenix to be held in May 1995. His heart leaped as he read the ad and his mind flashed back twenty-seven years to the dangerous and sorrowful mission he had performed. He sat down and wrote the note to Doc Quartuccio hoping someone at the gathering in Phoenix would remember the incident and help him to stop the nightmares of those men aboard PCF-19.

I was that someone and we spent several hours on the phone that day as we gathered our thoughts of that day long ago. I explained to Larry that I was aboard PCF-12 that night and we were the last people to see the crew alive. I knew a couple of the names and that two had been rescued but did not know where they were or where they were from. The SBSA had not yet been formed so there was no database of Swifties to look up, just the men I had met at the gathering in Phoenix.

Larry and I began a campaign that grew from he and I to the large base of witnesses that I have today. We gathered ships logs, message traffic, eye witness accounts, talked to the divers, even the squadron commander of the pilot blamed for the incident even though he was not there. Some very brave men were dishonored that night because they flew a mission to intercept these helicopters in the early morning hours of June 16th. On June 17th, they returned to the area and during the action they accidentally hit the USS Boston and HMAS Hobart killing two Australian Sailors. The evidence we have gathered points to enemy fire on the night of June 16th and although the two boards of inquiry decided it was "friendly fire" in the case of PCF-19, we do not know if they saw or reviewed all the evidence that we have. Thanks to the Internet and the Freedom of Information Act, this evidence is now in our hands and the true story of that night can be told through the eyes of the witnesses that were there. The Vietnam War is over but for many of those who were there that night, this book will explain why they have the nightmares and the belief in themselves that the truth can now be revealed. I will try to tell the story of each of the witnesses as told to me backed up with ships deck logs and message traffic.

I was able to explain to Larry all about Swift Boats, their layout, how the crew came to be where they were when the boat was hit, the various ratings serving on board and what they were doing near the DMZ on that night. I explained our weapon systems, radar and communications procedures, and how we conducted board and search operations in Market Time. He was able to understand why the bodies were in the positions found by the divers and why their clothing or lack of in some cases was determined by this information. The Vietnamese Sailor had his own identity card and one that he had taken from a fishermen when searching a sampan. He was fully clothed because he normally just laid down in the cabin during the night so he was available to act as an interpreter if needed. He did not stand a watch. The crewmen that were partially clothed in the forward cabin were off watch and asleep when the boat was hit. The crew locations were as follows; LTJG John Davis, OinC, was sitting by the port side door of the pilothouse. BM2 Anthony Chandler was behind the helm in the pilothouse. GMGSN John Anderegg was on lookout in the gun tub located atop the pilothouse. Bui Quang Thi was the South Vietnamese Navy liaison/interpreter lying on the lower bunk in the main cabin. QM2 Frank Bowman, an African-American, was asleep in the forward cabin. EN2 Edward Cruz, from Guam, was asleep in the forward cabin. GMG2 Billy Armstrong was asleep in the forward cabin. According to the divers, the boat was hit by two rockets, one of which entered just above the waterline on the port side below John Davis' position and exploded in the forward cabin killing Armstrong and Cruz. It is unknown the cause of death for Bui Quang Thi because his body seemed to be undamaged, possibly he drowned after being knocked about the cabin from the impact. Frank Bowman although badly wounded managed to climb out of the main cabin and on to the after deck where he swam free of the boat as it sank. Ltjg Davis remembers a flash of light and seeing Chandler stand straight up in the helm chair and then he was blinded. He remembers falling to the deck, which was now about ankle deep in water. The boat was sinking fast and he stood up and felt his way out of the open door and into the sea. He could hear sounds of the boat bubbling and gurgling as it settled in the water. PCF-19 sank in about four minutes. The divers reported the boat position as sitting on the bottom in an upright position. The rocket explosion was not very large and showed a penetration hole of approximately 76.2 MM, the size of a standard rocket carried by aircraft, not a missile. The explosion must have split the seams in the bottom and the boat simply settled in the water as the seas rushed in from the bottom. Another rocket hole in the engine room about the same size made a total of two rocket hits. Ltjg John Davis is swimming around, blinded and calling for help when he heard a familiar voice. It was John Anderegg, who had been blown clear of the boat by the rocket blast from his position in the gun tub. He was not severely injured and was able to see and swim to his skipper's side. He told him that the life raft had floated to the surface when the boat sank, triggered by the pressure release. He found Frank Bowman swimming toward it and helped him reach the life raft. Frank was badly wounded in the chest and was having trouble breathing. Anderegg was not certain of the extent of his wounds but wanting to search for other crewman that may have made it out, he told Bowman to hang on to the raft until he returned. He swam around the area of floating debris and diesel fuel and did not see anyone come to the surface. He heard John Davis' cries for help and swam toward the sound of his voice. Reaching his skipper, he told him about Bowman and swam with him toward the life raft. It was very dark with occasional light when the moon appeared from behind the clouds. It was very quiet when they reached the life raft and Frank Bowman still clinging to the raft. John Davis heard him talking to Bowman but could not see anything. Then Anderegg said, "I cannot hold on to him, he just died in my arms and slipped away." His widow Connie Anderegg Messenger told me in a phone conversation that her husband told her many times that he died in his arms and he could not hold on to him. His body has never been found and remains missing in action to this day.

Suddenly there was engine noise and shouts followed by lights as the USCG Point Dume, commanded by LTJG Ron Fritz, arrived on the scene. John Anderegg and John Davis were quickly pulled from the water. Davis slipped from their grasp and fell back in but was quickly retrieved. He still wonders today, who dropped him so he can thank him for saving his life. Once aboard Point Dume, their wounds attended to while the crew searched for more survivors.

Within a few minutes after the survivors were pulled from the water, PCF-12 arrived from its patrol area to the south and assumed the Enfield Cobra Alpha Patrol Area vacated by PCF-19. Information was quickly exchanged between LTJG Fritz and LTJG Pete Snyder on PCF-12 and the Swift Boat took up the search as Point Dume rushed to Cua Viet to deliver the two wounded crewmen to medical facilities inside the Cua Viet River. PCF-12 continued the search without finding any more survivors or any sign of Frank Bowman.

Communication was established with the Naval Gunfire Liaison Officer on the beach at Alpha One and the Marines at Ocean view as they had gone to alert status. Witnesses ashore saw the boat hit and manned their fighting positions while continuing to monitor the skies for more aircraft. Using their radar and IFF monitoring equipment they were able to determine friendly and enemy aircraft in the area. Reports of UFO's or unidentified flying objects (not alien spacecraft), which is an identifier for aircraft of unknown origin, had been filed for several nights prior to June 16th. There had also been reports of accelerated NVA troop movements along the DMZ. These UFO's were tracked as they moved between the Mainland to the north of the DMZ and Tiger Island, which is located a few miles offshore.

Larry Lail and I continued our search for evidence and information about the sinking using letters to Washington D.C. Archives. Larry located the reports of the crewman listing their cause of death and hometowns. He found the families and communication was established with them. Over the next several months and then years, Larry and I would find another piece of the puzzle and a new name of a witness. In each case, Larry would laboriously copy the pages of the evidence we had uncovered so far and send it to them. Phone calls and searches on the internet led us to many witnesses who related to us how this one incident had haunted them all these years and eagerly searched their memories and personal records to help us. By far the luckiest break came when Larry checked the membership of the Purple Heart Association, a National Organization of Combat Wounded Veterans. He found a John D. Davis listed in Niles, Ohio. He found a phone number and called him. John Davis had responded to a letter from the Purple Heart Association only a year before and had decided to join. He had returned to Ohio and became a teacher living out a quiet life with his family. His memories of his experiences on PCF-19 haunted him and nightmares were common. The call from Larry Lail took him by total surprise. They talked for a long time that night on the phone.

Larry Lail called me very excited to report his find. He gave me the phone number and the next night I called John Davis. After several questions, we established that he was the man we were looking for. We both shed some tears that night and as I recalled the events of that night from the deck of PCF-12, the memories came flooding back. I must say that John Davis began to come out of his shell that night, a shell that his wife Nancy reports made him sometimes distant and very sad. In the ensuing months and years, I have watched John become bright and vibrant at times and now willingly chat about his crew and his experiences in Vietnam. He gets sad sometimes, as we talk more about individual members of his crew and that night in June 1968, but smiles when remembering a detail about one of them. He was very proud of them and although suffering from "Survivors Guilt", I believe that this investigation has helped him resolve some of the issues that haunt him to this day. We have become the best of friends and talk frequently on the phone. He joined the Swift Boat Sailors Association and has attended many of the events and reunions. He enjoys the contact and friendship with his former comrades on Swift Boats. Through this contact, John continues to enjoy his senior years, which I believe are filled with a renewed sense of pride in his service. John believes hostile aircraft attacked him although he never saw what hit his boat. Through this account, I hope to state my case that his crew was indeed attacked by hostile forces not American Jets.

Our search continued with periods of no information for weeks followed by sudden "finds" of new evidence or another witness coming forward. One of these "finds" occurred as I was searching a veterans website that contained pictures of a former Marine Officer that had returned to Vietnam on a tour. He had been assigned to 1st Amtracs with the Marines and stationed near the DMZ in 1968. I saw a picture of an island taken as he flew over it on the way back to Hanoi to return to the U.S. from this tour. He commented that he did not know the island was there or what its name was. I sent an e-mail to him telling him that it was called Tiger Island and had been the focus of an incident I was involved in where a Navy Swift Boat had been sunk. He responded with "When were you there and what do you know"?

This began a series of communications, which included Larry Lail as we brought Richard Lennon up to speed on our search so far. He, too, had many questions about the incident and as we shared information, he was amazed to learn that much had happened at sea while his troops were involved on land. They were unaware of the sequence of events that unfolded out on the water. He was pleased to learn that others had sighted the helicopters as well although from a distance and using radar and night observation devices. He was introduced to John Davis and we set about planning a return to Vietnam and the sight of the sinking. Alex Radesa, a former crewman that had trained Frank Bowman when he arrived in country and knew John Davis' crew very well, joined our group. Richard did most of the planning having contacted the tour company that had handled his first return visit.

John Davis, Richard Lennon, Alex Radesa, and myself flew to Vancouver, B.C. just before Memorial Day in 1998 where we met at the airport. I had met John Davis but we all only knew each other from correspondence. We boarded a Cathay Pacific 747 for the long flight to Hong Kong and then Hanoi. We spent several days in Hanoi followed by a train ride to Hue and then by van to Dong Ha. We visited Khe Sahn, the Rockpile, Freedom Bridge and many other sites near the DMZ before heading to Cua Viet. We stayed at the lighthouse now built on the LST ramp on the river. We were able to walk the beach and get close to the site of PCF-19's hull, which still rests on the bottom of the South China Sea. Vietnamese troops barred us from continuing to the actual site but I believe we were within a mile of the site according to Richard's recollection of the landmarks. He found Oceanview and Alpha One, at least the locations; all evidence has been removed of the installations. After a short prayer for the crew of PCF-19, we returned to the lighthouse. After ten days in Vietnam, the four of us returned to our homes feeling much better for having gone. Unfortunately, Alex had many personal problems and ended up taking his own life soon after we returned. I do not believe the Vietnam trip contributed to this because he was upbeat and enjoyed the trip especially when he could interact with the children. He loved sharing candy and treats with them wherever we found them. It was a rewarding trip for all of us.

The search continued with locating John Anderegg's family and learning that he had been killed in an automobile accident in 1987. He left a widow and a daughter in Illinois whom we contacted for information. Although his death was a blow to our investigation because only he remembered the events of that night after PCF-19 was sunk while in the water, we have pieced together from John Davis' memory and Connie Anderegg Messenger, his widow. He received a Purple Heart as well as the Silver Star for his actions on the night of June 15/16th 1968. The rest of the crew's families received Purple Hearts Posthumously as well. This in itself is significant because Purple Hearts are not normally awarded for "friendly fire" injuries and Silver Stars are only awarded for action against the enemy and only for Valor or Heroism. It is not an award that is given lightly.

I placed a post on the website of USS Boston and have a website of my pictures from Vietnam. Both have generated responses, which I have followed up in person or via e-mail. Space forbids me to account them all but the most significant will be related here in this book using their permission.

CHAPTER TEN

Witnesses and Their Accounts of the Events of June 15/16th

O ne of the men on post that night was Cpl. John B. (Andy) Anderson with B Co. 1st Amtrac Battalion (Reinf) 3rd Marine Division. In a report of his experiences while in Vietnam for the Marine Archives in August 2004, Andy relates his sightings of these UFO's from his post at Oceanview.

JAN 68 AT OUR NEW OBSERVATION POST AT "OCEANVIEW" I WAS NOW EITHER WITH A CO OR 2/4 CAN'T REMEMBER THAT'S SGT BOHRER IN BACK RADIO TECH GUY IN FRONT WAS ARMY INFANTRY ADVISOR ON NEW GROUND SENSING DEVICES AND STARLIGHT SCOPE WE GOT CALLED DOWN TO MY LOC FROM HERE UGH! NEED HELP WITH OTHER TWO GUYS.

Figure 8. CPL John B.(Andy) Anderson and others on station.

He was a radio operator and moved between the base at C-4 and Oceanview. I am quoting from his report:

"I continued to go on patrols with B Co. and BLT, especially south of C-4 and out into the desert. We made trips up to Oceanview a lot and I was attached there at the top of the hill for three months with brief trips back to C-4 and Cua Viet. They also got ground radar at C-4. I was sent back to Oceanview for a short term with a CO. and witnessed the chopper incidents. Sgt Boherer and I always seemed to end up at Oceanview. We went to Oceanview this time to man COC with radio watch and new SUPERNOD scope. (Authors Note: By Andy's time frame in his report it would be early May 1968) They eventually had some tanks up there as well as some xenon searchlights. Oceanview did not look the same anymore although my little bunker/hooch was still there. A lot of us slept outside under the stars on top of the hill. Now this is when we started seeing lights a lot. (UFO's) in the night sky above the "Z" going back and forth from Tiger Island and we saw a lot of them! We had seen them earlier with Bravo Co. and they were determined to be UFO's. They usually had red and white blinking lights under them and were large enough to be clearly seen from our position even without the starlight scope. We also saw a lot of "floating" lights. I never knew what they were as they looked like floating balls of light. We even got reports of these back at Cua Viet from night guard posts at B Co. We watched them for a couple of weeks when it was decided that they were a type of cargo ship that was harmless.

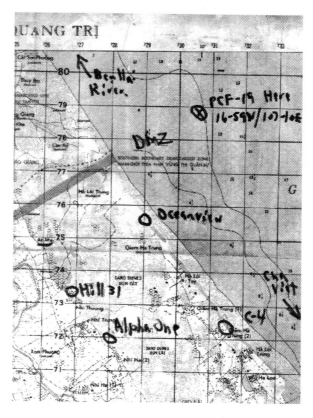

Figure 9. Topo Map showing the Marine Unit location near DMZ.

Cpl. Gammons called in a report one night that he had seen what looked like a "fast train" moving across the "Z". We were usually in contact with "Dagmar Delta" at the north bank of the river as well as the "Enfield Cobra" Swift boats that routinely went up and down the coast to the East of us. The coast was clearly visible except for a small line of trees to the Northeast, which hampered our view of the immediate coastline. We could see the remaining coast all the way to Tiger Island and the bend around the Ben Hai River, which concealed the entrance to the river somewhat. I remember an Army Sgt. from 1st Cavalry who was some kind of spotter and had been sent up there to help set up the Starlight Scope and to man COC observation. He thought we were all crazy about these choppers even as they were flying in plain sight, lights blinking like hell. I think he had a Cpl. (SPC4) with him. I have a photo of him but no name. Lt. Richard Lennon (Authors Note, He was XO of A Co. 1st Amtracs) does not remember any Army personnel being there and maybe he had left by then and was there with B Co. Anyway, we saw the flash of rocket fire coming from one of those choppers to the Northeast and learned that PCF-19 (Enfield Cobra Alpha) had been hit. It was off and on cloudy that night but one minute that boat was there and then it wasn't! I think they sent out a squad to survey the beach in the morning and they found debris, etc. I heard in the Seabee Club all about this later and Sgt. Boherer and I would say, "I told you there were choppers up there, we saw them in April and May"! I talked to Major D.L. Stefansson (Authors Note, He was in Command of S-3 Company, 1st Amtracs and Cpl. Anderson was his radio operator a various times while at the forward positions) about this and he said he had seen one mistakenly fly over the CP at Cua Viet and hightail it back North. He also told me, as he was Battalion S-3 at the time that Saigon had sent up Army personnel to discount our sightings, even going to the point of accusing us Marines of "smoking funny cigarettes"! Unquote.

Cpl. John (Andy) Anderson's report was a summary of his tour in Vietnam sent to USMC Archives and the previous section was a part of this report. After he had made contact with me in July of 2004, he had contacted Major Stefansson asking him for his advice on giving me his statement for this book. In an e-mail from Major Stefansson to Andy, he gives this account and I quote.

"I would let him read the accounts. I too saw one of the NVA choppers up real close. The damned thing flew over the Cua Viet River one afternoon. I am convinced that the pilot thought he was flying the Ben Hai until he saw the U.S. flag flying over Task Force Clearwater. He then made a fast left turn and headed north as fast as possible. Speculation was the NVA helos were flying artillery weapons and ammunition to Tiger Island in anticipation of the USS New Jersey coming on station.

I have seen pictures of the missile cases found on the USS Boston. There is no doubt that they are U.S. missiles slung on jet fighter/attack aircraft.

It was reported to Division, but like many things, I don't think we were believed. When we first reported seeing helos at night, an Army team from Saigon flew up to Battalion and took our observers into "custody". They tried to break their report, even accusing them of being influenced by funny cigarettes. I found the visitors from the South to be disgusting.

I had another encounter with these "visitors" after one of our forays into the DMZ. The intelligence finds were extremely valuable, but the BG (Brigadier General) from Saigon was more interested in doing head counts of the forces that we sent across the line to ensure that we hadn't sent more than 100. What rubbish". Unquote.

From the Headquarters 1st Amphibian Tractor Battalion (Rein), 3rd Marine Division (Rein) FMF, Command Chronology for period 1 June to 30 June 1968 sent from the Commanding Officer to Commandant of the Marine Corps (Code A03C), comes the following excerpts;

In the Narrative Summary;

1. Elements of the battalion located at Oceanview, YD 293754, sighted numerous unidentified flying objects believed to be helicopters. The majority were sighted in the vicinity of the Ben Hai River and toward Tiger Island, YD 483987. To assist in positive identification, the battalion elements at Oceanview were provided with two Xenon Searchlights and after many attempts, the searchlight crew illuminated one twin rotor helicopter on 19 June 1968.

In the List of Significant Events;

An entry on 1 June 1968 states that Co "B" at C-4 position, is using PPS-5 Radar and NOD or Night Observation Device to detect enemy troop movements in the DMZ at night.

15 June 1968   UFO's in vicinity YD 2674, YD 2582 and YD 2583, Reported by Blurry Critic "L". All towers alerted And makings. UFO's appear to be helicopters. Notified CO and put BN on blackout status.

16 June 1968   4th Platoon, Co "A", at Oceanview, reported UFO's In their area firing air to ground missiles and that Swift Boat which they were observing by means of NOD (Night Observation Device) had disappeared. Through monitoring Swift Boats freq, confirmed that one Swift Boat is missing.

Co "B" reports observing 10 UFO's; 5 in Tiger Island vicinity, 2 in peninsula area, 2 north of Hill 23 and one in Con Thien area. Elements of Co "B" at Oceanview, observed 5 UFO's; 2 in area of Tiger Island and 3 Northwest of Oceanview.

Fire Raider NGF Spotter Team, at Oceanview, and at the Tower at Amtrac CP, reported one UFO hit by Naval Aircraft.

Platoon Leader, at Oceanview, believes the Swift Boat was sunk by fixed wing aircraft. He says he observed rocket flashes and moments later the Swift Boat disappeared.

4th Platoon, Co "A", at Oceanview, reports finding wreckage of Swift Boat and one MIA.

The reports above are in chronological order by day however the exact times are not listed. Since the first sightings were at the end of the 15 June and the beginning of 16 June summaries, it can be ascertained that they occurred just before midnight on 15 June and between 0001 and daylight of 16 June 1968. There are two other entries unrelated to this incident that appear to have occurred during the daylight hours of 16 June followed by this last entry that says;

> Co "A" reports what appears to be UFO activity from the mouth of the Ben
> Hai River to Tiger Island.

This is significant because the attack on PCF-19 occurred just after midnight on June 15th and before 0100 on June 16th, as indicated in the records and logs. The attacks on USS Boston and HMAS Hobart occurred about the same time on 17 June, 24 hours later. These attacks as sighted by witnesses and recorded in logs will be addressed when I discuss the events of 17 June.

Witnesses to the incident continue with the USCG Point Dume (WPB 82325) commanded by LTJG Ronald E. Fritz, USCG. This 82-foot craft was on routine patrol off the DMZ and had the call sign of Enfield Cobra Victor Alpha. According to her deck log,

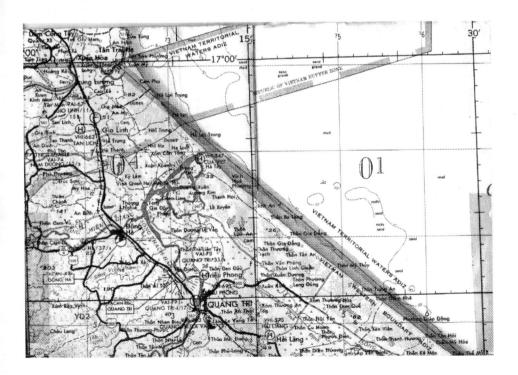

Figure 10. Navigation Chart of Quang Tri to DMZ Area

which when signed by the Commanding Officer of a Naval Vessel is a legal record and can be used as evidence in a Court Martial, Point Dume was underway in the South China Sea on Market Time Patrol in Area 1A1.

According to the deck log for June 15th, Point Dume had rendezvoused with USCGC Campbell and taken Commander Coast Guard

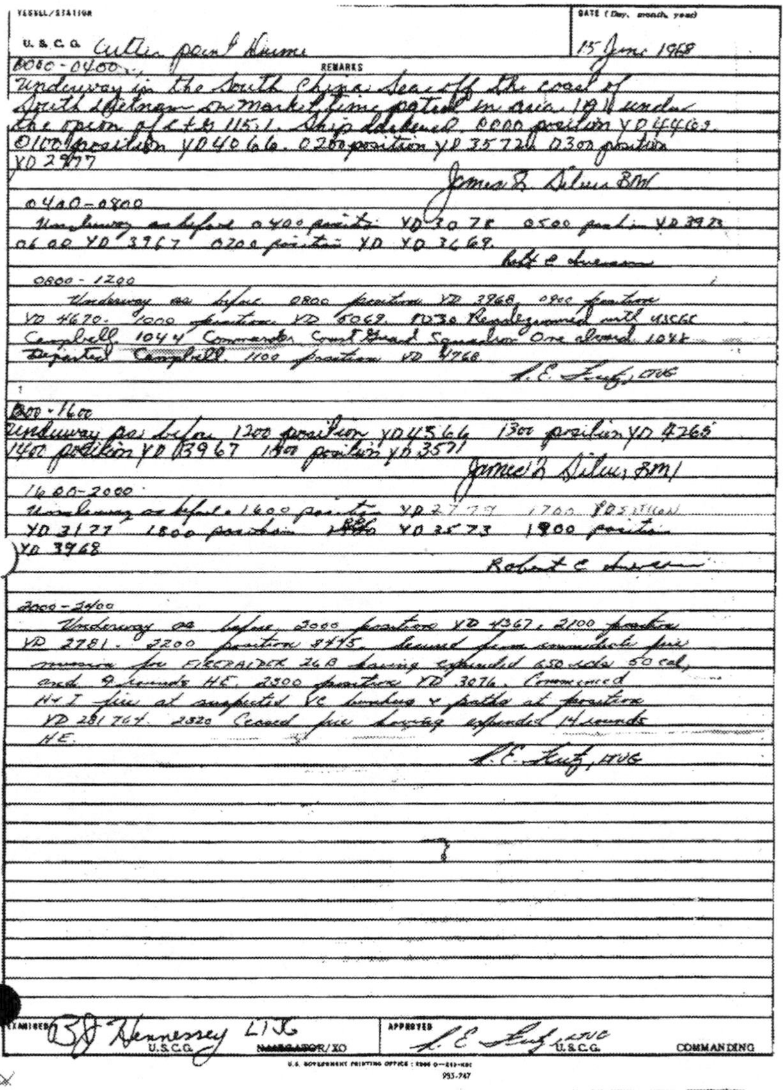

VESSEL/STATION
U.S.C.G. Cutter Point Dume

DATE (Day, month, year)
15 June 1968

REMARKS

0000-0400
Underway in the South China Sea off the coast of South Vietnam on Market Time patrol in area 1A1 under the opcon of CTG 115.1. Ship darkened. 0000 position YD 4469. 0100 position YD 4066. 0200 position YD 3572. 0300 position YD 2977
James R. Silver BM1

0400-0800
Underway as before 0400 position YD 3078 0500 position YD 3973 0600 YD 3967 0700 position YD YD 3669.
Robt C Swenson

0800-1200
Underway as before 0800 position YD 3968. 0900 position YD 4670. 1000 position YD 5069. 1030 Rendezvoused with USCGC Campbell. 1044 Commander Coast Guard Squadron One aboard. 1048 Departed Campbell. 1100 position YD 4766
R. E. Fritz, LTJG

1200-1600
Underway as before 1200 position YD4366 1300 position YD 4265 1400 position YD 3967 1500 position YD 3571
James R. Silver, BM1

1600-2000
Underway as before 1600 position YD 2777 1700 position YD 3177 1800 position YD 3573 1900 position YD 3968
Robert C Swenson

2000-2400
Underway as before 2000 position YD 4367. 2100 position YD 2781. 2200 position 3475. Secured from immediate fire mission for FIRERAIDER 26B having expended 650 rds 50 cal. and 9 rounds HE. 2300 position YD 3076. Commenced H+I fire at suspected VC bunkers + paths at position YD 281764. 2320 Ceased fire having expended 14 rounds HE.
R. E. Fritz, LTJG

EXAMINED B. J. Hennessey LTJG U.S.C.G. NAVIGATOR/XO
APPROVED R. E. Fritz, LTJG U.S.C.G. COMMANDING

U.S. GOVERNMENT PRINTING OFFICE
953-747

Figure 11. USCG Point Dume Deck Log for June 15th, 1968 (Courtesy of Ron Fritz, CO of Point Dume).

Squadron One aboard. Later that night she would respond to an "immediate fire mission" for Fireraider 26B expending 650 rounds of 50 cal and 9 rounds 81MM HE ammunition. This was at 2200H and her position was YD 3375. From 2300 to 2320, she fired Harassment and Interdiction Fire of 14 rounds 81MM HE at suspected VC bunkers and paths at position YD 281764. Moving away from this position having completed this mission, Point Dume resumed normal patrol. Her position at 0001 16 June 1968 was YD 3772.

Figure 12. USCG Point Dume, an 82-foot cutter at her berth in Danang.
(Picture courtesy of Mark Bell)

At 0100 Informed by Fireraider 26B (Authors note; this was the Forward Air Controller at Alpha One) that Enfield Cobra Alpha appeared to have been hit and was smoking, Underway max speed enroute scene. 0120 Arrived on scene, ECA appeared to have been sunk. 0130 Retrieved two personnel from water—LTJG Davis and GMGSN Anderegg, continued searching debris for other survivors.

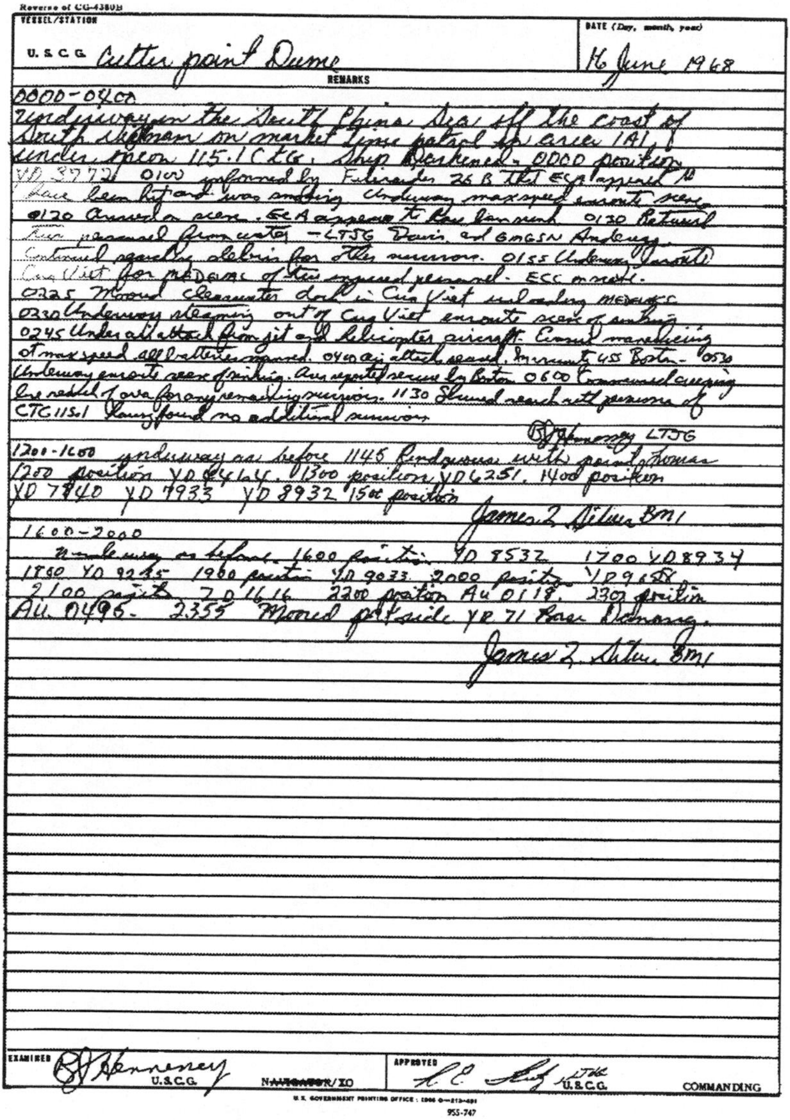

Figure 13. June 16th, 1968 Deck Log of USCG Point Dume
(Courtesy of Ron Fritz, CO of Point Dume)

Underway, enroute Cua Viet for MEDEVAC of two injured personnel. Enfield Cobra Charlie (PCF-12) enroute. 0225 Moored Clearwater dock in Cua Viet unloading MEDEVAC 0230 Underway steaming out of Cua Viet enroute to scene of sinking. 0245 Under air attack from jet and helicopter aircraft. Evasive maneuvering at max speed, all batteries manned. 0400 air attack ceased, in vicinity USS Boston. 0530 Underway enroute to scene of sinking, area reported secure by USS Boston 0600 Commenced creeping line research of area for any remaining survivors. 1130 Secured search with permission of CTG 115.1 having found no additional survivors. 1200-1600 Underway as before. 1145 Rendezvous with Point Thomas. Point Dume then departed for Danang mooring portside to YR-71 at 2355. She remained there until the Board of Inquiry convened at which several of her crew testified. On 23 May 1969 Point Dume was awarded the Meritorious Unit Commendation for her part in the rescue of the PCF-19 crewmen.

Further witnesses continue with a statement written by LTJG Pete Sullivan, the Naval Gunfire Liaison near the scene. He testified before the Board of Inquiry and wrote the following statement:

I, Ltjg Pete Sullivan USNR, having been informed by RADM S.H. Moore, USN of the matter under investigation and having first been advised of my rights under Article 31 of the Uniform Code of Military Justice, do hereby voluntarily make the following statement:

I am assigned to the 12th Marines and work in the 3rd Division FSCC located at Dong Ha as a Naval Gunfire Liaison Officer (NGLO). In order to gain an understanding of the problems of the marine spotter in the field, I volunteered to go the Alpha One, an observation post located at 16-5GN 107-08E. On 24 May, I arrived at Alpha One and commenced studying the terrain, calling in fire missions and in general familiarizing myself with the duties of a naval gunfire spotter.

On 15 June at approximately 2200, the spotter on watch began awakening all personnel in the bunker stating that there were aircraft in the area and that "Beach Boy 26 Oscar" had stated the craft were "definitely unfriendly". I dressed and went directly to the observation post on top of the hill. The man on watch using all the methods of surveillance available sighted a number of blinking lights in the sky. These lights were observed by the naked eye, with low power binoculars, and with a night observation device. Approximated thirteen were in view at that time. Most of the lights were northeast of A-1 position in the vicinity of the east-west ridgeline north of the Ben Hai River. Other lights were heading south on both our east and west. Those to the east were three in number, two of which appeared to go as far south as the Cua Viet River. Those to the west went approximately the same distance south. Judging from the speed of the lights and the manner in which they hovered on occasion, they appeared to be helicopters. There was an occasional high-speed light that appeared to be a jet plane. At no time could I hear the sound of a helicopter engine. Occasionally, a jet would pass over or near A-1. When the red light pulsated a superstructure could be seen on the slow moving UFO's but the luminescence was insufficient to determine shape or form of aircraft.

Some time after midnight, I saw two white projectiles travel in a direction of southeast to northwest over a low trajectory and impact either on the shoreline or just off the coast. Range perception was difficult due to darkness. Shortly thereafter, no more than thirty seconds, I heard a jet aircraft pass by A-1 heading from east to west. Fire Raider 26 Bravo called my station i.e. American Beauty 26 Charlie and inquired if I saw the projectiles and he reported seeing them himself.

Shortly after this, illumination rounds were fired in the area of the impact of the projectiles; the illumination was definitely at sea. At this time Fire Raider 26 Bravo stated she was going off the net for 05 minutes. 26 Bravo remained off the net considerably longer those five minutes, perhaps as long as twenty to thirty minutes. 26 Bravo returned to the net and requested that MEDEVAC's be sent to the area. Later 26 Bravo reported friendly small craft engaged in rescue operations while receiving small arms fire from north of 26 Bravo's positions. From A-1, I observed fifty caliber tracer rounds being fired from northwest to southeast. It appeared that land based small arms were firing out to sea. Range perception was difficult and the tracers may have been fired from a sea-based position. Other tracers were fired from a position south of Fire Raider 26 Bravo. The tracers traveled from southwest to northeast and also seemed to be firing at an object at sea. Though I knew they were in the area, I couldn't see the friendly boats.

Fire Raider 26 Bravo called in a naval gunfire mission against the enemy to his north but he was put in check fire because of friendly aircraft in the area.

The blinking lights remained in the sky to the north at this time and sustained their activity until daybreak.

On the evening of 16 June, the pulsating lights appeared again and remained visible until shortly before daybreak. They were concentrated north of the Ben Hai River and seemed to be shuttling back and forth along the ridgeline north of the river. Others seemed to shuttle from the mainland to Tiger Island.

These craft did not come as far south on this second evening though three or four did pass down to positions east and west of A-1.

At no time did I observe the aircraft with the blinking lights fire on a target. This statement was handwritten by Pete Sullivan and dated 21 June 1968. I have talked with Pete concerning this report which he provided to me and he said that during his testimony at the Board of Inquiry, he was asked repeatedly if he saw any helicopters clearly enough to identify them. He said he did not. Pete Sullivan is from Somerville, MA.

LTJG Peter B. Snyder, OinC of PCF-12, submitted the following Combat After Action Report to the Board of Inquiry at Danang.

THIRD ENDORSEMENT on officer in Charge PCF 12 Ltr of 24 June 1968

From: Commander Coastal Surveillance Force (CTF 115)
To: Commander, U.S. Naval Forces, Vietnam

Subj.   Combat Operation After Action Report

Ref: (a) PCF 24 191445Z JUL 68
        (b) PCF 24 200230Z JUL 68
        (c) COMSEVENTHFLT 180246Z JUN 68

Forwarded concurring with the First and Second Endorsements.

2. No intelligence concerning hostile A/C in the vicinity of the DMZ was available at any NAVFORV level. The attack on PCF-19 appears to have been the first indication of any possible enemy air activity south of the DMZ.

3   There has been a considerable amount of message traffic generated concerning identification and command control subsequent to the sinking of PCF-19 and attacks on PCF-12 and Point Dume. Action and remedial policies have been promulgated of procedures to be taken when under attack. However, all procedures promulgated thus far are of the "after the fact" type and will not prevent initial attack on friendly surface units. References (b) and (c) cite an incident on 19 July whereby 10 VS's were killed by a U.S. Air Strike over water south of Coastal Group 14 base (BT 235515). This strike was called in by an Air Force FAC and indicates that serious coordination problems still exist.

4. It is noted that in spite of several messages from higher authority (such as reference (d)) casting doubt on the creditability of helicopters sighted in the basic correspondence and on EIGHT subsequent occasions by TF 115 PCF's and WPB's) that OINC of PCF 12 remains adamant in his original report that helicopters (unqualified) were in fact seen firing on PCF 12. This statement of sighted hostile helicopters firing on PCF 12 and POINT DUME remains fully supported by the CO and one senior PO of PT DUME. Although CTF 115 subsequent messages 030840Z JUL 68, 121415Z JUL 68, 121641Z JUL 68, 122059Z JUL 68 and 222221Z Jul 68, there is much less evidence supporting the doubt implied by reference (d). Accordingly, CTF 115 will continue to report airborne lights or sightings resembling the characteristics of helicopters (otherwise not identified as "friendlies") as BOGIES to COMSEVENTHFLT and other required operational commanders.

5   The action taken by the OINC and crew of PCF 12 was timely, correct, and commendable.

R. F. HOFFMAN

Downgraded at 3-year intervals;
Declassified after 12 years

Figure 14. Third Endorsement on Officer in Charge PCF-12 Ltr of 24 June 1968.
(Courtesy of Peter B. Snyder, OinC of PCF-12)

The four pages Combat After Action Report follow courtesy of Peter B. Snyder, OinC of PCF-12:

From: Officer-in-Charge, PCF-12
To: Commander Northern Surveillance Group
Via: Commander Coastal Division TWELVE

Combat Action After Action Report (U)

(a) NAVFORVINST 3480.2A of 20 OCT 1967

In accordance with reference (a), the following combat after action report is submitted:

a. Name or Identify/And/Or/Type of Operation: Market Time Patrol

b. Dates of Operation   151130H JUN – 161130H JUN 1968

c   Location: Tonkin Gulf and adjacent beach vicinity YD-340740, Quang Tri Province, RVN

d. Control or Command Headquarters: Commander Coastal Surveillance Force (CTF 115)

e. Reporting Officer: LTJG Peter B. Snyder, USNR, 696165/1105

f. Task organization: Single units under the command of Commander Northern Surveillance
    Group (CTG 115.1)

g. Supporting Forces: USCGC Pointe Dume

h. Intelligence: All types of offensive weapons were know to be within the capability of enemy
    forces due to the proximity of this area to North Vietnam. The area under discussion is area 1A1,
    which extends from the 17th parallel, about 10 miles South. Within this area, the enemy has
    initiated attacks on Market Time units using artillery, rockets, recoilless rifle, automatic weapons
    fire, and sniper fire from shore. Reports of junks infiltrating South from the Ben Bai River have
    been substantiated by sightings and attacks on junks by USA and USCG units. The Combat After
    Action Report of PCF-81, serial 026 of 7 March 1968 and USCG Debriefing Report of 22 April
    1968 refer. The coastline in this area is straight sandy beach with dunes and tree line immediately
    behind the beach area. The sea area has been declared restricted to all civilians on a 24-hour
    basis by the Government of Vietnam. The enemy held Tiger Island is 16 miles to the Northeast
    of YD-4898. Although this island does not fall within the area under discussion, it does rate
    mentioning due to its potential as a possible base of operations for North Vietnamese military
    operations. Intelligence in this area is adequate insofar as land operation are concerned.
    However, this is the first instance of USN or USCG Naval surface units ever having contact or
    combat with North Vietnamese air units in this area. Intelligence of the presence of North
    Vietnamese Aircraft in the area had not been received by Coastal Division TWELVE or this unit.

i. Mission: Preventing the infiltration of man and ammunition from the sea.

j. Concept of Operations: Patrol the coast of South Vietnam with small craft

Figure 15. Combat Action Report Page One.

The second page follows:

Subj: Combat After Action Report (U)

(PCF or WPB) to detect infiltration both visually and by radar.

k.   Execution: While patrolling in 1C, south of area 1A at time 0110H, 16 June 1968, the OINC of this unit overheard a transmission on circuit S-9 from Fire Raider 26B (a land based spotter north of Cua Viet) to Enfield Cobra Victor One (ECV1), the USCG Point Dume, that Enfield Cobra Alpha (ECA), PCF-19, had received a rocket attack from seaward and had sustained two hits. At this time, this unit was in the southern sector of its patrol area 1C. It should be noted that this unit had casualties to the URC-56 and the VRG-46 radios. Both units were inoperative and only the PRG-25 emergency radio was operable. All radio communication was via this radio. At 0120, Point Dume confirmed that PCF-19 had been hit and that it had been sunk. Point Dume noted that the area was full of debris from the stricken PCF. This unit tried to contact Point Dume and the offshore Picket Ship E6Z (USCG Cambell) but had negative results. At 0135, Point Dume said that she had picked up the survivors holding onto the PCF's life raft, one in bad shape, the other fairly well off. Point Dume radioed for illumination. Fire Raider 26B replied that he might help. At that time, this unit got communications with Point Dume and Fire Raider 26B and told Point Dume where this unit was and when we could be on the scene to assist in illuminating the area for him. From this time, this unit had good communications with both Point Dume and Fire Raider 26B throughout the night. At 0150, this unit arrived on the scene, YD-303793, and immediately provided 81mm illumination for Point Dume. At 0155, Point Dume departed the area for Cua Viet to MEDEVAC the two survivors. Point Dume informed this unit that the survivors were the OINC and the GMGSN and that 4 more were unaccounted for. This unit continued to illuminate the area and search for more survivors. The area was strewn with bits and pieces of mattress, paper, paint chips and oil. At 0200, this unit received from FR-26B that there were Helo A/C in the area and they were not friendly. At that time, the crew was already in full battle dress and the boat at Condition ONE. No Helo A/C were spotted and FR-26B was notified of this fact. With the guidance of FR-26B this unit continued to illuminate and search the area. At 0210, this unit spotted two Helo A/C with flickering (blinking) lights overhead, altitude +2,500 feet. The A/C were hovering. FR-26B was immediately notified. This unit discontinued use of 81mm illumination and utilized the moonlight, estimated to be 30% illumination. The two Helo A/C either turned off their lights or left the area as this unit lost sight of both. Speed of this unit at this time was 5 knots. At 0225, this unit received a single rocket attack from seaward, at a low trajectory, which passed 2 feet over the main cabin from starboard to port and exploded in the water 10 feet from the port side. Negative casualties or damage. Immediately, this unit turned toward the direction of the attack to present as little target as possible and to bring the forward twin .50 caliber mounts to bear, increased speed to maximum and commenced firing on a Helo A/C hovering at 1,000 feet with lights blinking. Helo A/C then began to increase altitude rapidly. This unit notified Point Dume and FR-26B of the attack. FR-26B then stated that any A/C in this area were unfriendly. This unit did not turn on identification lights after the attack

Figure 16. Combat Action Report Page two.

The third page follows:

Subj: Combat Action After Action Report (U)

As per operation Order since we had been previously notified of unfriendly Helo A/C in the area. At 0235, this unit received what seemed to be 40 – 50 rounds of .50 caliber tracer fire from the beach area North of the Cua Viet River. All rounds fell astern. It should be noted that this unit was still south of the 17th parallel and that it was over 4 miles from the North Vietnamese coast. This unit believes that the hostile fire to have originated from a Helo A/C at a low hover above the water, using the coast as camouflage. This unit suppressed the tracer fire with .50 caliber and 7 rounds HE VT 81mm. This unit again notified Point Dume and FR-26B. From 0240 to 0355, this unit and Point Dume were under constant air attack from all angles by Helo and fixed wing A/C. Gunners we4re ordered to fire the .50 caliber guns at any and all air contacts, lighted or unlighted. Point Dume and this unit commenced evasive steering at maximum speed at the USS Boston (CAG-1) which was 7 miles seaward of this unit. This unit was unable to enumerate the number of runs made by Helo A/C during that time, however, there were more than enough to keep both gunners and all others firing continuously for 75 minutes with .50 caliber and M-16 weapons. One time during these attacks, this unit was overflown by jet aircraft at 1,500 feet after it had just completed a firing run at Point Dume. It is believed that the tracer rounds form the jet fell down the port side of Point Dume. This unit was not attacked by the jet. The aircraft was seen by the after gun mount personnel and had a stovepipe type fuselage and sweptback wings. The jet came from the South and then proceeded North and was not seen again. Tactics used by the Helo A/C were one of two kinds. Primary was the tactic where lights were turned off and the strafing runs began. However, once the lighted Helo A/C was spotted, it could be followed without lights. The secondary tactic used was hovering at a high altitude and quickly descending to a hovering position of a few feet above the water and firing short bursts at the PCF. This tactic may have been used to rocket PCF-19. At 0355, this unit was advised by FR-26B that friendlies were in the area. Personnel at this unit were instructed to cease firing. They were then instructed by the OINC to fire only if fired upon. This unit then proceeded to take station 1,000 yards to the landward side of the USS Boston. Point Dume joined this unit soon after.

Results: There were no personnel casualties or apparent damage to this unit as a result of the air attacks. Enemy A/C never were able to close this unit closer than 250 yards as a result of the .50 caliber fire.

m. Special Techniques: The tactic of evasive steering at high speeds is essential in attacks of this nature. The major disadvantage of his tactic is the illumination caused by the stern wake at high speeds. Also used to good advantage was the placement of one extra man on the pilothouse roof next to the forward gun tub as a spotter. It increased the effectiveness of the forward twin .50 caliber guns to a large degree.

n. Lessons Learned: PCFs can engage helo A/C and repel attacks in a firefight. The slow relative speed of the Helo A/C at altitudes of 100 – 1,000 feet

Figure 17. Combat Action Report Page three.

The fourth and final page follows:

Subj: Combat After Action Report (U)

Makes it very possible for .50 caliber gun to follow and hit such a target with consistency. The fact that no Helo A/C successfully completed a run on this unit or Point Dume bears this out. The presence of only a 100 round ammunition magazine on the after .50 caliber considerably decreased the volume of fire from this gun due to frequent reloading. The use of the 81mm mortar utilizing VT fuses as an anti-aircraft weapon is too slow to load and train to be of any good.

o. OINC's Analysis: Helo A/C attacks on naval surface units in the I Corps area has presented a new aspect to PCF warfare and tactics. The fact that one PCF was destroyed bears out that such attacks can and are successful when the element of surprise is utilized. An unlighted Helo A/C at high altitude overhead at night is almost impossible to spot from a PCF. In this firefight, Helo A/C used lights in positioning themselves. This gave the PCF crew enough warning and target to fire upon. Attacks of this sort are much more effective on nights of little natural illumination as was the illumination this night (30%). From silhouette and profiles of these attacking Helo A/C were of the Russian "Hound" class. It should be noted that Fire Raider 26B did an outstanding job of locating enemy A/C as they began their strafing runs on ECVl and this unit. The information they passed to us was invaluable. This unit wishes to express its deep gratitude to this very competent group of men. The most blatant and serious inconsistency has been saved for last. Never did this PCF or any other PCF/WPB unit get any advance intelligence on hostile helo or fixed wing A/C in the area prior to departing on patrol. With the vast complex of intelligence media available, it is hard to conceive how events like this could happen. The first information of enemy A/C in the area came from Fire Raider 26B, moments before the attacks.

p. Recommendation:

Ensure that intelligence concerning hostile A/C in vicinity of Market Time patrol areas is disseminated to all pertinent Market Time activities and units.

2. That permanent CAP be provided in the area of the DMZ.

3. That the magazine on the after .50 caliber mount be enlarged to hold 800 rounds vice the 1000 rounds already there.

4. That close liaison with forces ashore by Market Time units continue to be emphasized.

Very respectfully,

Peter B. Snyder

Figure 18. Combat Action Report Page four.

In this report LTJG Peter Snyder relates the actual events as seen by himself in the pilot house, the actions he took as OinC of PCF-12, and his recommendations to the chain of command for future incidents of this nature involving these unknown aircraft. This report was submitted although he did not testify before the board of inquiry. Several members of Point Dume's crew did testify as well as LTJG Peter Sullivan, the Naval Gunfire Liaison Officer. Members of the PCF-12 crew testifying were QM3 Gary Rosenberger, the helmsman at the time and myself. Gary told the board that he had observed an unlighted fixed wing aircraft fly over PCF-12 at low altitude but it did not fire on us. After reviewing several aircraft silhouette cards, he identified one as the aircraft he observed. It was listed on the card as a Russian built MIG-21. I was called in to describe the aircraft that had appeared ahead of PCF-12 and while hovering above the water, began to fire machine gun rounds at our boat. I described the aircraft to an artist who drew a sketch of this aircraft and when completed, I testified that it was indeed what I saw. It was identified as a MI-4 Hound Class Helicopter of Russian design. It is listed in Jane's Fighting Aircraft as a cargo/troop helicopter with an armament of air to surface rockets and a single machine gun. A picture from the newspaper is shown here except it is a side view.

Russian Copter Called Viet Target

an MI-4 helicopter hove   e army source said three MI-4 heli-   more Sunday near the Demilitarized Zone
e in Moscow. A S. Vit   copte s were shot down Saturday and   in South Vietnam. (Story on Page a-1)

Figure 19. A News clipping from Stars and Stripes.
(Courtesy Stars and Stripes and from my files).

This is a picture and description of the same aircraft from Jane's Fighting Aircraft.

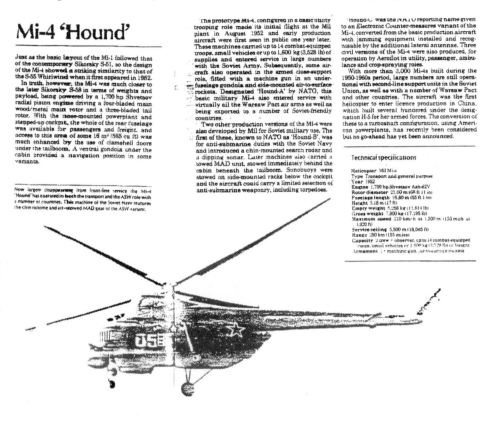

Mi-4 'Hound'

Just as the basic layout of the Mi-1 followed that of the contemporary Sikorsky S-51, so the design of the Mi-4 showed a striking similarity to that of the S-55 Whirlwind when it first appeared in 1952.

In truth, however, the Mi-4 was much closer to the later Sikorsky S-58 in terms of weights and payload, being powered by a 1,700 hp Shvetsov radial piston engine driving a four-bladed main wood/metal main rotor and a three-bladed tail rotor. With the nose-mounted powerplant and stepped-up cockpit, the whole of the rear fuselage was available for passengers and freight, and access to this area of some 16 m² (565 cu ft) was much enhanced by the use of clamshell doors under the tailboom. A ventral gondola under the cabin provided a navigation position in some variants.

Now largely disappearing from front-line service the Mi-4 'Hound' has operated in both the transport and the ASW role with a number of countries. This machine of the Soviet Navy features the chin radome and aft-stowed MAD gear of the ASW variant.

The prototype Mi-4, configured in a basic utility trooping role made its initial flight at the Mil plant in August 1952 and early production aircraft were first seen in public one year later. These machines carried up to 14 combat-equipped troops, small vehicles or up to 1,600 kg (3,528 lb) of supplies and entered service in large numbers with the Soviet Army. Subsequently, some aircraft also operated in the armed close-support role, fitted with a machine gun in an under-fuselage gondola and side-mounted air-to-surface rockets. Designated 'Hound-A' by NATO, this basic military Mi-4 also entered service with virtually all the Warsaw Pact air arms as well as being exported to a number of Soviet-friendly countries.

Two other production versions of the Mi-4 were also developed by Mil for Soviet military use. The first of these, known to NATO as 'Hound-B', was for anti-submarine duties with the Soviet Navy and introduced a chin-mounted search radar and a dipping sonar. Later machines also carried a towed MAD unit, stowed immediately behind the cabin beneath the tailboom. Sonobuoys were stowed on side-mounted racks below the cockpit and the aircraft could carry a limited selection of anti-submarine weaponry, including torpedoes.

'Hound-C' was the NATO reporting name given to an Electronic Counter-measures variant of the Mi-4, converted from the basic production aircraft with jamming equipment installed and recognisable by the additional lateral antennae. Three civil versions of the Mi-4 were also produced, for operation by Aeroflot in utility, passenger, ambulance and crop-spraying roles.

With more than 3,000 Mi-4s built during the 1950-1960s period, large numbers are still operational with second-line support units in the Soviet Union, as well as with a number of Warsaw Pact and other countries. The aircraft was the first helicopter to enter licence production in China, which built several hundred under the designation H-5 for her armed forces. The conversion of these to a turboshaft configuration, using American powerplants, has recently been considered but no go-ahead has yet been announced.

Technical specifications

Helicopter Mil Mi-4
Type Transport and general purpose
Year 1952
Engine 1,700 hp Shvetsov Ash-82V
Rotor diameter 21.00 m (68 ft 11 in)
Fuselage length 16.80 m (55 ft 1 in)
Height 5.18 m (17 ft)
Empty weight 5,268 kg (11,614 lb)
Gross weight 7,800 kg (17,195 lb)
Maximum speed 210 km/h or 1,500 m (155 mph at 1,320 ft)
Service ceiling 5,500 m (18,045 ft)
Range 250 km (155 miles)
Capacity 2 crew + observer, up to 14 combat-equipped troops, small vehicles or 1,600 kg (3,528 lb) of freight
Armament 1 × machine gun, air-to-surface rockets

Figure 20. This is the better picture of the aircraft that I observed tracking and firing on PCF-12. (Courtesy Jane's Fighting Aircraft).

There may have been others that testified before this Board of Inquiry held in Danang, but I am only aware of these.

One of the contacts sent to me via e-mail from Richard Lennon, was John Taylor, a former LTJG who served aboard USS Boston and involved a website in Australia. It was titled Gunplot and was all about the Royal Australian Navy and contained a section on Vietnam and the incident of June 17th, 1968 when HMAS Hobart was struck by American missiles with the loss of seven crewmen. John Taylor had contacted Richard Lennon responding to an article on the Internet he wrote following our trip to Vietnam in 1998. This was in August of 2000 and he recalled the attack on Boston and Hobart and reflected the same belief that both hits and PCF-19 were on the same night. This is similar to the accounts of that time in which the same jets that hit Hobart are blamed for PCF-19. It seemed like an easy way to explain away the enemy helicopters and the press and general public did not question it.

Boston received a near miss from the missiles from the same aircraft and received minor damage. His report is on the Australian website and mine is there as well. I did this because like many accounts of this incident, the attacks on PCF-19, Hobart, and Boston are implied as being the same night and they are not. This website has generated many more contacts and witnesses as well. John Taylor has sent me much information including copies of the deck logs from June 16/17 as well as a book of the Boston put together by him. It documents the entire period he served aboard Boston and was very helpful in my search. His connections also led to more contacts and evidence and I value his friendship highly although we have never met.

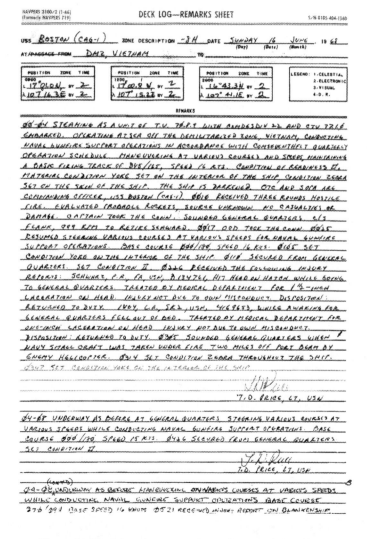

Figure 21. Deck Log for June 16th, 1968 from USS Boston.
(Courtesy LTJG John Taylor).

I begin John Taylor's reports by quoting from his book which details Boston's period on the gunline in mid June 1968. On June 6th, Boston embarked Captain K.J. Cole COMDESDIV22 and staff and departed Subic Bay with HMAS Hobart (DDG-39). On June 9th, Boston rendezvous with USS Boyd (DD544) on station at Point Betty near Hue. June 10th, refueling from USS Sacramento (AOE-1 at sea. (Authors note, RD3 Mike Stowe is aboard USS Boyd and was a witness covered later in this chapter) June 11th Boston joined TU 77.1.2 Sea Dragon Ops off Dong Hoi, North Vietnam with USS Saint Paul (CA-73) and USS Theodore E. Chandler (DD-717). (Authors note, RM3 Jim Fitch is aboard USS Chandler and was a witness covered later in this chapter). Fired at targets located at various "Choke Points" interdiction points North of DMZ where roads, highways, and rail crossings intersect. June 13th Boston rearms at sea from USS Paracutin (AE-18) off the DMZ. June 15th, after several months standing watches in the engine room, Ensign John Taylor is moved to Combat Information Center to learn to be a Gunfire Liaison Officer. These (GLO's) work with Fleet Marine Force Air/Naval Gunfire Liaison spotters attached to the fire support bases, with USAF Forward Air Controllers (FAC's), Army Air Observers (AO's) or directly with Fire Support Coordination Centers. Just after midnight of June 15/ 16th, as cited in the Boston Deck Log, Boston is steaming off the DMZ as a unit of TU 70.8.4 with COMDESDIV22 and CTU 77.1.0 embarked. At 0010 Received three rounds hostile fire, evaluated probable rockets, source unknown, no casualties or damage. Captain took the Conn. Sounded General Quarters. Flank Speed to retire to seaward. Resumed steering various courses at various speeds for Naval Gunfire Support Operations. At 0110 Secured from General Quarters. At 0305 Sounded General Quarters when Navy Small Craft was taken under fire two miles off port beam by enemy helicopter. Boston remained at General Quarters until 0426. (Authors note, This small craft was PCF12).

As shown in the above account from Boston, she and the ships with her were not far from the coastline when this attack occurred. Major Richard Lennon, ashore at Oceanview remembers sighting the helicopters flying in formation between the mainland north of the Ben Hai River out to sea with their lights on as observed by the starlight scope. The starlight scope was a night observation device that used the available light rather than infrared to see objects. It was very effective in extreme low light situations giving a soft green glow to objects in range. Aircraft lights, a cigarette, and other low intensity lights sources showed up very clearly in this device. An aircraft flying close by with lights or an illumination flare would be so bright as to show up as a smear of light. Exposing this device to daylight ruined the scope and it was kept below in its case during daylight hours. It came as a riflescope, a larger hand held and a crew served, mounted size. The latter was used at Oceanview and Alpha One. One of the memories that I have of the Ben Hai River area at night is the stark contrast between the often-lit up skies to the south as observed from sea on a Swift Boat. Looking to the south as we patrolled off the entrance to the Ben Hai River, numerous lights from aircraft and illumination flares hanging in the sky along with tracer fire from Marine guns and aircraft attacking NVA targets all along the DMZ area. Sometimes the exchange of green and red tracers along with the bursts of fire from larger weapons created an eerie background at night. Sometimes a flash of light from seaward followed by a loud noise would indicate one of our Naval Ships firing its guns at targets far inland or just along the coast. As I observed the area north of the Ben Hai River, it appeared to me as if a dark black curtain had been drawn covering the north as far as we could sea. Swift boats would sneak in around midnight close to shore and using the starlight scope, observe troops moving along the beach and sometimes sampans hugging the shoreline moving supplies and people toward the DMZ area. On several occasions, an 81 MM Mortar fire illumination round lit up the area as we moved a mile or so off the beach. These targets were taken under fire with 50 caliber machine guns and mortars, as this was "free fire zone".

I describe this to indicate the type of scenario faced by the Marines from Oceanview and Alpha One at night. It was easy to see the helos flying out to sea and back again against this backdrop of darkness to the north. If they were south of their positions, the background of flares and gunfire would hide these small lights. For the Swift Boats and the Coast Guard WPB's on patrol, the nights were spent in an uneasy awareness of how close the enemy was. Most of the time up there was spent at General Quarters, guns and lookouts manned because we were in range of many NVA weapons such as recoilless rifles and rocket propelled grenades. It was standard procedure to notify the Marines and FAC at Oceanview and Alpha One of our intention to sneak up north to try and catch the NVA attempting to move material southward. It was also standard to check in with them periodically by radio to make sure they knew where we were at all times. These were not covert operations, just standard Alpha Patrol operations at the DMZ. Ltjg John Davis and PCF-19 were just coming back from one of these operations up north when they were hit. They had been observing the lights moving out to sea and back but they were farther north than PCF-19's location. She was steaming in a southward direction. Cpl John Anderson and Cpl Ken Anderson with the Marines as radio operators were watching the northern area of the DMZ and coastline area and talking on the radio to Point Dume and one of them insists he was talking to Enfield Cobra (Victor) Alpha when a hovering aircraft fired two rockets that exploded on the sea. The communication and the visual sighting of PCF-19 were gone. This was between 0030 and 0100 approximately. In the later hours PCF-12 coming under attack along with Point Dume would repeatedly ask for confirmation that the aircraft flying around them were friend or enemy. The answer was given, "no friendlies in the area", as FAC's and Air Force Command Structures scramble to account for their aircraft especially those that might have been returning from missions over North Vietnam. During this time all requests to fire on these aircraft were denied. When the "hovering" aircraft near PCF-12 and Point Dume showed threatening maneuvers and began to fire machine guns at them, the response was to return fire and maneuver out of the area.

During this time, Mike Stowe, an RM3 assigned as forward lookout aboard USS Boyd (DD-544) was noticing all this firing and activity near the beach. His ship was approaching the DMZ from the south and saw a lot of star illumination flares being set off over the water, which he thought was strange. He saw a flashing red light like the type on the belly of an aircraft flying along close to the beach and at one point saw orange tracers coming from the aircraft shooting towards the water. He says he thought this "idiot pilot" must have been flying along with the red light going to attract attention to identify targets. At the speed the aircraft was flying, it had to be a chopper. The next morning when he went on watch he was advised of the incident with the Hobart and the PCF. He does not recall exactly the date whether it was June 15/16 or June 16/17th. As stated before, the news reports following these events and the official statements tended to merge the two events together and they clearly were on separate nights with Hobart and Boston hit by missiles on June 16/17. It was just after midnight on both nights and therein lies some of the confusion in reporting. It appears that higher commands wanted to give the impression that both events were related once the decision had been made to declare it "friendly fire".

Major Richard Lennon with the 1st Amtracs at Oceanview recalls reporting the choppers over the north before midnight of June 15/16 and suddenly all hell breaking loose as the radio nets became alive with calls and reports. Sometime before midnight an air strike was called in response to the helos even though they had not moved south in a threatening manner. It was very quiet over the DMZ that night prior to this time and even the NVA troops and their guns had been quiet for the most part. He heard but did not see two jets fly over heading northward and as they approached the helos, their lights went out only to reappear again this time closer to the water. They seemed intent on their mission of traveling back and forth to a point out to sea. Richard did not know at this time about the island off shore known as Tiger Island. It appears low on the horizon but was not visible to the Marines from their visual point at Oceanview. It was during a return visit to Vietnam in 1996 that he learned about the island and when he saw it for the first time he noticed that it seemed much farther south almost straight out to sea from Oceanview. He had heard rumors that they had been resupplying the island in preparation for the arrival on station of USS New Jersey (BB-62) in the fall of 1968. When he visited Cua Viet and talked with the keepers of the lighthouse now built on the LST ramp, he learned a different story. The lighthouse keeper, who grew up in this area, told him the island was a training and drop off point for swimmers, who would swim into the Cua Viet River and place mines on the supply ships and craft moving material up from Danang. One theory expressed to my witnesses is that PCF-19 and maybe PCF-12 as well stumbled on one of these swimmer drop off missions using the NVA Helicopters.

Further information on IFF gear and radars came to me from Thomas M. Steinberg, RD2 aboard Boston. He was in charge of the air picture on both June 15/16 and 16/17, 1968. I asked him to explain these radar capabilities and IFF since the problem was blamed on poor equipment and communication between Naval and Air Force Units. He said the following:

USS Boston was equipped with and AN/SPS-30 and an AN/SPS-48 radars. The SPS-30 was long-range height finder and the SPS-48 was a long-range 300-mile radar.

IFF with PIF was a transponder on the aircraft once turned on it was activated by ship borne equipment for ID. It should be noted that mode 3 and 4(pif) were coded. Now on a good day we could get radar and IFF as far away as 250 to 270 miles. We held IFF at longer distance sometimes longer than radar contact.

In a war zone no aircraft were allowed to fly if their IFF was not working. The reason being they could not be ID'ed and thus were to be shot down. I did forget to mention that all capital ships had the same equipment (IFF) as aircraft. This was so the aircraft would not shoot at us. If no IFF, it was a free target.

Therefore it can be determined that Boston had a good view of the air picture and the friends and foes in it. She reported to PCF-12 that the aircraft were not squawking IFF meaning they were not friendly. John Taylor stated that the Terrier Missile System aboard Boston was antiquated and slow, barely able to track fast moving jet aircraft however it appears the IFF equipment and tracking radars were up to the task. On the June 16/17 incident when Hobart and Boston were hit by missiles, the incoming aircraft were tracked and ID'ed as friendly aircraft and thus were not fired on. Not so for the June 15/16th aircraft which also moved much slower than jets and appeared to hover at times.

It has been theorized that the two F-4 Phantom Jets that appeared over Ocean View just before midnight of June 15/16th and were directed to the moving lights above the Ben Hai River were responsible for the sinking of PCF-19. They were from the 366th Tactical Fighter Wing (TFW) based in Danang.

It is said that they looked down their radar and fired at the Swift Boat thinking it was a NVA Helicopter since the Swift did not have an IFF transponder and appeared to be not a friendly contact on their radar. The problem with this theory is the size of the holes in PCF-19. According to the divers that dove on the wreckage on June 16, 17, and 18 the entry holes were just above the waterline on the port side. The holes resembled those of an air to surface unguided rocket similar to those carried on helicopters such as the MI-4 Hound as well as U.S. Helicopters.

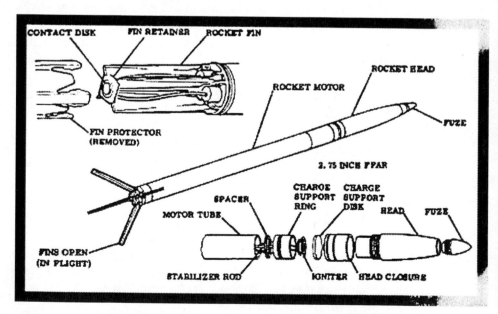

Figure 22. Exploded view of an unguided rocket carried on helos.

There were two entry holes and no exit holes indicating the warhead exploded inside the forward cabin spreading shrapnel everywhere. A missile such as the AIM-7 Sparrow and other air-to-air missiles do not make a hole like this and the explosion is far different than these small rockets. The charge on a Sparrow spreads a net of metal mesh designed to cut through the skin of an aircraft and damage the turbine engine and controls causing it to spin out of control and crash. It has a proximity fuse that causes the explosive charge to detonate close to but not hitting the target. The other missiles carried were AIM-9 Sidewinder air-to-air missiles. This weapon has a point-detonated warhead that uses the heat signature of the aircraft's engine to home in on. The Swift Boat's heat source is the engine room and the rockets did not aim for the engine room rather the forward cabin area.

Figure 23. F-4D Phantom Jet over North Vietnam.
(Courtesy Navy Photo Files).

The F-4D Phantoms had a gun pod that was mounted externally on the centerline for ground support and some air combat missions. It was a SUU-23 pod containing an M-61A1 20 MM cannon. It is unknown whether the F-4's over the DMZ that night carried this weapon. The later F-4E Phantom Aircraft came with this cannon on board.

Major Richard Lennon USMC was the Executive Officer of Co. "A" 1st Amtracs which had just relieved Co. "B" up at Ocean View on June 15th. He had gone up to Ocean View to see LT Peter Schneider the platoon leader, Ken (Andy) Anderson was his radio operator. It was on this first evening that they first saw the lights moving above the Ben Hai River. They were picked up on a super starlight scope. A radio call was made back to Battalion at Cua Viet and all hell broke loose. There were communications all the way south to Division Headquarters in Quang Tri and then somewhere even higher than that. He says he was talking to PCF-19 when the two aircraft scrambled from down south, probably Danang. He was helping the aircraft locate the target lights as they flew over their positions when a flash of light and explosion to seaward of their position followed by a loss of communication with the boat. He was unaware of any more activity to seaward until he and I made contact many years later. He said the next morning there was a lot of debris on the beach from the boat and he thought a body but could not confirm it. In the succeeding days, many visitors from upper command and the media would arrive asking questions. A tank was brought up to this position with a special outfitted xenon light mounted on it. It was buried in the sand during the day to hide it from the North Vietnamese gunners and uncovered at night where it was set up facing the north. The plan was to illuminate the helos with this high intensity light to get a visual identification. However, when the lights appeared over the river in the succeeding nights, and the tanks light was turned on them, they turned out their lights and no visual sighting could be made. This action even drew Henri Huet, the famous French AP photographer, however he went away disappointed as well. These lights proved to be as illusive as ever. Some of Richard Lennon's men were sent back to the rear areas and questioned until they wondered if they could believe what they saw. Some were accused of being drunk and smoking "funny weed" causing them to see these lights.

They weren't the only ones seeing them for sure because the swift boat crews up on the DMZ for several days after this and even into August reported these lights and their strange path back and forth to Tiger Island. They were tracked on radar and visually sighted by the lookouts on the Navy ships along the DMZ but only at night. No one ever reported a close up sighting of the helos except PCF-12 and apparently the higher commands did not believe them either, at least not officially.

On June 20th, 1968, a message went out from COMCRUDESGRP SEVENTH FLEET to RUHHHQA/CINPACFLT, INFO COMUSMACV SAIGON, RVN, CINCPACAF, SEVENTH AF, III MAF DANANG, RVN, AND COMSEVENTH FLEET. SUBJECT; INTERIM FINDINGS OF FIRING INCIDENTS.

I quote from this message:

A. CINCPAC 180715Z JUNE 68

1. In compliance REF A. RADM S.H. Moore, USN, assisted by COL M.J. Quirk, USAF, SEVENTH AIR FORCE, COL R.C. Lehnert, USMC, III MAF, and CAPT W. Wright, USN, CHIEF OF STAFF CCD-2, has conducted preliminary review of various events occurring between 15-17 June in the DMZ area with respect to helicopters and the attacks against ships and craft in general vicinity of DMZ. Although time limitations and complexity of situation have not permitted conclusive findings regarding all incidents, following interim report is submitted.

2. Enemy helicopter activity vicinity DMZ remains inconclusive. To date, of the limited number of personnel interviewed who were on-scene, most were insistent that definite helicopter activity occurred in the DMZ area during hours of darkness. Further, most of those interviewed stated that hostile fire was received from helicopters. Helicopter identification determined primarily on sightings of lights moving in a manner to suggest helicopter flight characteristics, however, no hits attributed to helicopter attacks have yet been reported and no other confirmation of visual sightings has been obtained.

3. The following is summary of firings against Navy and Coast Guard Ships and Craft during the hours of darkness 15-17 June.

B. At 160010H8 USS Boston in fire support area Bravo (vicinity 16-58 N0 107-15E4) reported receiving what appeared to be three rounds rocket fire from direction of south portion of DMZ. Immediately after firing, Boston lookout reported unlighted jet overhead. Prior to attack, Boston reported fast moving radar contact showing no IFF. Investigation reveals one USAF F-4 (Gunfighter 05) launched two AIM-7E Missiles on heading 060" from vicinity 17-DIN9 107-03E3 at 060010H8. Strong possibility exists that Gunfighter 05 inadvertently launched attack against Boston.

C. Between 160030H and 160100H (exact time undetermined) PCF-19 under fire by what was reported to be two rocket rounds and was sunk at 16-59N1 107-10E9. Rounds received on port side while on a southerly course. Underwater photos confirm hits on port side. No identifiable ordnance fragments recovered. Subsequent demolition PCF-19 precludes further investigation of hulk. Investigation revealed two USAF F-4 (Gunfighter 03 and 04) expended four AIM-7E missiles and 220 rounds 20MM ammunition during the period 160042H3 and 160055H7. Position of Gunfighter 03 and 04 at the time of firings not yet determined. Investigation continuing.

D. Between 160225H6 and 160355H0 PCF-12 and USCGC Pt. Dume vicinity 16-56N8 107-12E1 were reportedly under repeated attack by both jet aircraft and helos. No damage sustained. No report of friendly airborne ordnance expenditure during this period. Investigation continuing. Unquote.

Notice that Gunfighter 03 and 04 expended four missiles and 220 rounds of 20MM ammunition during the time PCF-19 was hit, however the skipper of Point Dume on the scene did not hear or see any cannon fire. The sound is unmistakable. He observed lights flying around but did not hear the jets when PCF-19 was hit although it was in his sight. Both the Marines ashore and LTJG Ron Fritz report the area was unusually quiet prior to the attack. Ltjg John Davis of PCF-19 says he did not hear any sound prior to the hit but he had observed the helo lights earlier using the starlight scope. He and his crew had taken PCF-19 into North Vietnamese waters, as is the common practice in this area in an attempt to catch the enemy smuggling arms and material along the beach with sampans. This technique has paid off in good intelligence and occasionally catching the enemy off guard by illuminating them and taking them under fire. No prior permission was required since it was a free fire zone. The Swift Boats and Coast Guard WPB's would cover each other and kept in contact with the Marines and Forward Observers when performing this mission. This night was like any other night on the DMZ, dark and quiet and very dangerous. The crew of PCF-19 knew what they were doing and had followed all procedures.

There is more to this message but it involves the next night and the attacks on Hobart and Boston.

Another message dated 250354Z June 68 to the same addressees provided the following additional information. I quote:

Helicopter Incidents

Ref A. COMCRUDESGRU SEVENTHFLT 201650Z JUNE 68 NOTAL (This is the message printed in part above)
Ref B. COMCRUDESGRU SEVENTHFLT 231616Z JUNE 68 NOTAL

1. Interim reports of investigation subject incidents reported by Refs A and B to CINCPAC are summarized herein:

   A. Evidence of enemy helicopter activity vicinity DMZ remains inconclusive, most personnel interviewed were insistent that definite helo activity occurred during the hours of darkness. Such opinions were based on sighting lights rather than actual helos. No hits have been reported from attacks attributed to helos. Tentative indications are there is no evidence of coordinated attacks on Pt Dume and/or PCF-12. And that jet passes on these units were by US Aircraft.
   B. U.S. Medevac helos were airborne enroute to and from USS Repose from 160315H6 to 160340H4. Helos originated Quang Tri. Pilots stated no hostile fire observed during flight. No helos from ships operated in vicinity Boston during period of concern.
   C. No reports of friendly aircraft under attack correlate to times of ship firings.
   D. Accounts indicate all ship/aircraft IFF operating properly.
   E. No evidence available of enemy comm. deception reporting helos. Unquote.

As can be seen by the above message, by the 23rd of June, more evidence had been presented to the board but still they could not explain what hit PCF-19 or fired on Pt Dume and PCF-12. There were no friendly aircraft near us, nor do they hover, nor did they have machine guns. F-4 Phantom jets did not carry the type of rocket believed to have hit PCF-19 and was fired at PCF-12. If the jets had hit PCF-19 as they assumed, why were there no missile fragment found on board the PCF or more damage to the craft found. When these same missiles hit Hobart they killed two crewmen and caused major damage to this large cruiser. Boston received a near miss and damaged its superstructure leaving large pieces of the missile lying on the deck. They were large enough pieces that serial numbers could be read. Nothing resembling this amount of damage was found by the divers on PCF-19.

Richard Lennon would locate another major piece of this puzzle when he located the Squadron Commander of the 480th Tactical Fighter Squadron, (TFS). The 480th TFS was part of the 366th Tactical Fighter Wing (TFW), all of which were referred to as "Gunfighters". The Commander of the 480th was Colonel Don Damico and it was one of his pilots that returned from the mission with a helicopter kill. He was put in for a Silver Star but then the reports came in of the hits on PCF-19 and the next night, Hobart and Boston. The celebrations turned to sadness when this report was released. "Friendly Fire" is such an ugly term especially when you are the cause of it. Most incidents are thoroughly investigated before the findings are released and the party involved is usually disciplined unless it is ruled as "an accident" that could not be prevented. History shows these incidents to be uncommon where gross communications errors and equipment malfunctions are to blame. In this case it could have been missiles that went wide of the target and struck the boat but again we are faced with the explanation of the way a Sparrow Missile functions and the damage it causes. Both of which do not fit the profile of PCF-19's damage. It is often said, "That in combat, things are very chaotic and mistakes are often made". For those who have served in combat especially flying in supersonic aircraft, things happen very fast and targets approach very quickly. However, these aircraft and the pilots that fly them are equipped to think, react, and execute their actions in split second precision because that is the way they are trained. It takes special people to fly these aircraft and split second decisions can mean life or death in the skies. This is why I feel so strongly that a missile from an F-4 Phantom did not hit PCF-19.

As stated earlier, about 0330 a flight of F-4's flew over Point Dume and PCF-12's position headed north to engage the helos. No further contact was made between Point Dume, PCF-12 and the "hovering aircraft". Both boats moved to seaward near the Navy Ships in order to clear the area of friendly units. As dawn broke over the South China Sea, the crew of PCF-12 would reflect on all that had happened since we received the call just after midnight. We cleaned up the spent brass from the forward and after machine gun mounts and restowed loose gear tossed about in action. We were low on ammo, fuel, and exhausted from the stress of the previous five hours. PCF-12 would go alongside USS Boyd DD-544 and receive fuel and 50-caliber ammunition. Daylight brought a new look to the patrol area as Enfield Cobra Alpha resumed her patrol. Moving to the area where we spent time earlier searching for our friends, the currents had cleared the area of debris leaving a slick of fuel. This is all that remained of PCF-19 and her crew. Each man would reflect on those men lost that night in their own way depending on their relationship with them. I did not know the crew well being new in country, but I remember those moments to this day when EN2 Ed Cruz and I climbed down in the engine room and hooked up the jumper cables. I often wonder how that encounter between two enginemen would have developed and the friendship that began that night, had he not been killed. I liked Ed Cruz right off and I still see his face sometimes when I reflect on that night so long ago. Shock has a way of setting in slowly when this happens and our crew kept busy stowing our gear and trying not to reflect on our loss. There was time to grieve after we returned from this patrol. We were still on patrol in a hot area and as we moved closer to the Ben Hai River mouth, it was with a heightened sense of awareness that the enemy could strike swiftly and with deadly consequences.

About 0900, a radio call from PCF-101 told us that our relief was on the way. A call to Point Dume informed her that we were headed south to Danang. PCF-12 would rendezvous south of Hue and PCF-101 took over Enfield Cobra Alpha. Returning to our base, we learned from other Swifties, how the night went for them. Ltjg Bernard Wolfe in PCF-69 was Enfield Cobra Charlie Mike, just below us, and they listened carefully to the radio traffic, knowing that if PCF-12 was hit, they would be next to go north. They had already moved up to Enfield Cobra Charlie to replace us, as did all the Swift Boats on station down to Danang. The mood around the APL and the Repair Barge was very somber as everyone felt the loss. There had been casualties before; it is a part of the war we fought. The only details known at this time was that one of our boats had been attacked, that it was believed to be an aircraft from North Vietnam, and that five of our comrades were missing. A memorial service was held but I believe I was on patrol because I do not recall attending one. Within the next few days, members of our crew were to testify before the Board of Inquiry and then it was back to patrol duty. I would not learn until much later that "friendly fire" was blamed for the incident. I heard about Hobart being hit the next night and I thought it was helos that struck her as well.

Ltjg Bernard Wolfe would reflect in later years that he returned from R & R a few weeks after this and had a strange encounter at the Danang Air Terminal. An Air Force Major was standing in line in front of him and noticed his Swift Pin on the pocket of his uniform. He turned and asked, "Were you in one of those little boats we attacked a couple of weeks ago?" He said that he flew F-4's and they were sent on a night mission covering the "Alpha" area. They were told that anything located therein was to be considered hostile and attacked. Bernard gathered that he might have been of those that sank PCF-19. He asked "Why the hell were you in there?—The word had been put out on this". I explained what happened including Pete Snyder's observation that helicopters were involved. He replied, "No, it was probably us". On the other hand, Pete Snyder's observation of a helicopter attack was pretty convincing.

This account by Ltjg Bernard Wolfe and his encounter with the USAF Major attests to the confusion following the investigation and I believe the subsequent explanations to the various commands as to what really happened up there. For those of us at the other end of the chain of command, the war went on with new dangers to face each day from a hidden and dangerous enemy. In addition, the war had taken on a new and dangerous twist for those of us patrolling along the DMZ, both Navy and Marines. The lights moving above the DMZ continued to be seen and reported for several months after this but they remained as elusive as before remaining north of the DMZ.

CHAPTER ELEVEN

Sunday June 16ᵗʰ and the Aftermath of Tragedy

In the early morning hours, as the ships and Marine Units ashore pondered over the new developments of the nighttime action off the DMZ, USS Acme (MSO-508) received an unusual message. She had been on Market Time operations near Danang and was ordered to proceed to the Cua Viet area north of her position. There she would use her sophisticated sonar to locate the wreck of PCF-19, recover the bodies, and retrieve the publications and code books still on board. Since the area was just a mile and a half off the beach and less than five miles from North Vietnamese territory, Acme would be within range of the North Vietnamese shore batteries. These same guns pounded Cua Viet nearly every day. Cua Viet was well in the range of these guns. To protect Acme during her mission, she would witness jet aircraft from carriers and land-based airfields flying close support missions into the northern half of the DMZ and the nearby mountains. There was an armada of naval ships standing offshore with their guns ready and the crew of Acme became aware that something very big was happening.

HM1 Larry Lail was the corpsman assigned to the USS Acme and he was no stranger to this assignment although the rest of the crew would be. Larry Lail had served two tours before this as a Fleet Marine Force corpsman and had worked in the triage at Danang's base hospital. His job would be to examine the bodies of the crew as they were brought up and list injuries and identification markings such as tattoos, scars, etc.

Merlin K. Overholser, LCDR, USN commanded USS Acme. Acme was a wooden hulled ocean-going minesweeper designed to clear harbors and open sea areas of mines. She had special sonar that would be used to pinpoint the wreck of PCF-19 quickly to enable divers to recover the remains and destroy the wreck. Since the events of the earlier hours of darkness were still fresh in everyone's minds, the threat of another attack from these helicopters was very real.

According to the Deck Log of USS Acme for June 16ᵗʰ, 1968, she was on Market Time patrol and had been searching junks near Danang in Area Two. Excerpts from the deck log shown below are reprinted here for clarity. I quote from the deck log.

0600 C/C (changed course) 308 Underway for Area 1A1 in accordance with CTG 115.1 15214Z June 68. 1411 Went to General Quarters. 1443 PCF-101 came alongside our starboard quarter. Four divers came aboard from PCF-101; LTJG Stryer, BM1 Midgley, DP1 Feller, SA Johnson. 1446 Cast off PCF-101. 1522 Secured from General Quarters. 1612 Maneuvering on various courses and various speeds while engaged in sonar search. 1649 Obtained sonar contact 1704 Placed a Dan buoy to make contact. 1705 Away the motor whale boat with divers aboard to investigate sonar contact. 1710 Obtained another sonar contact identified to be PCF-19.

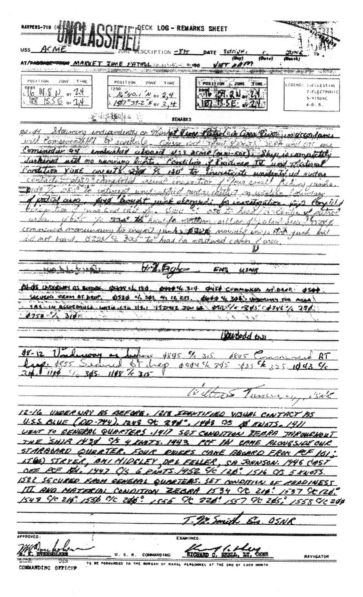

Figure 24. USS Acme Deck Log, June 16th, Page One.

(Authors Note: The results of the first contact were not known, however, it was a contact and Larry Lail believes it may be the wreck of a helo. It was not checked although subsequent searches picked up this contact on other days.) 1715 Motor whaleboat repositioning Dan buoy. (This was to move the buoy from the first contact to the second which was PCF-19) 1738 divers searching the sunken PCF-19. 1740 A P-4 float fixed to the wreck for identification. 1745 Commenced maneuvering at various courses at various

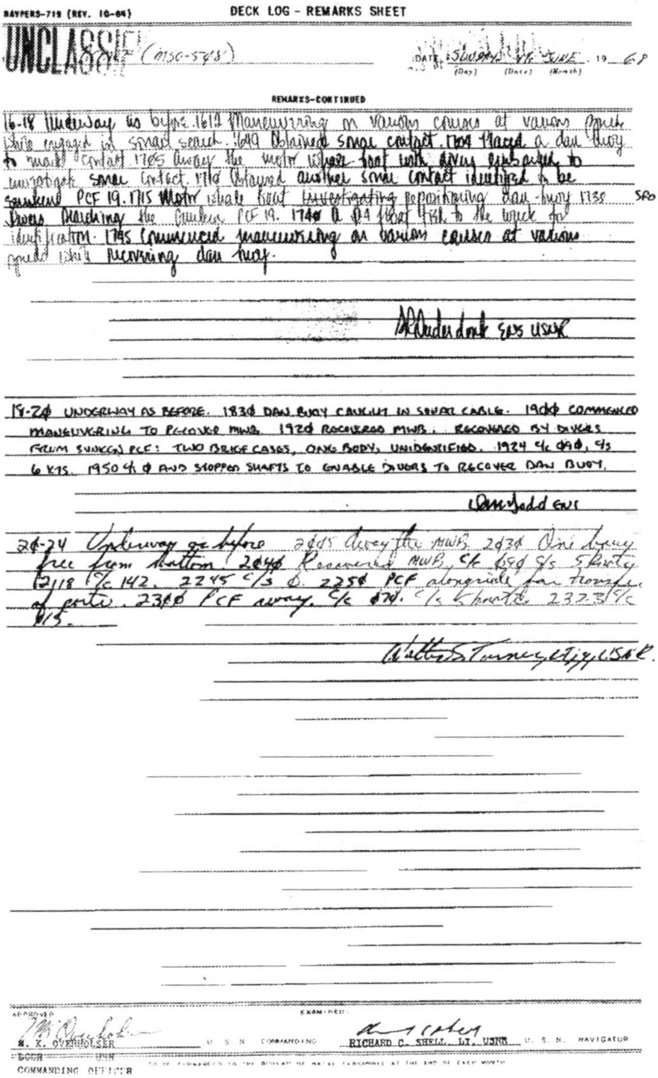
NAVPERS-719 (REV. 10-64) DECK LOG - REMARKS SHEET

UNCLASSIFIED (MSC-5?8) DATE Sunday 16 June 19 68

REMARKS-CONTINUED

16-18 Underway as before. 1617 Maneuvering on various courses at various speeds while engaged in sonar search. 1649 Obtained sonar contact. 1704 Placed a dan buoy to mark contact 1705 Away the motor whale boat with divers embarked to investigate sonar contact. 1710 Obtained another sonar contact identified to be sunken PCF 19. 1715 Motor whale boat investigating repositioning dan buoy 1738 Divers searching the sunken PCF 19. 1740 a P4 float fixed to the wreck for identification. 1745 Commenced maneuvering on various courses at various speeds while recovering dan buoy.

18-20 UNDERWAY AS BEFORE. 1830 DAN BUOY CAUGHT IN SONAR CABLE. 1900 COMMENCED MANEUVERING TO RECOVER MWB. 1920 RECOVERED MWB. RECOVERED BY DIVERS FROM SUNKEN PCF: TWO BRIEF CASES, ONE BODY, UNIDENTIFIED. 1924 C/C 090, C/S 6 KTS. 1950 C/S 0 AND STOPPED SHAFTS TO ENABLE DIVERS TO RECOVER DAN BUOY.

20-24 Underway as before 2005 Away the MWB. 2030 One buoy free from bottom. 2040 Recovered MWB, C/C 090 C/S 5 Knots 2118 C/C 142. 2245 C/S 0. 2250 PCF alongside for transfer of parts. 2300 PCF away. C/C 070. C/S 5 knots. 2323 C/C 015.

APPROVED: M. K. OVERHOLSER LCDR USN COMMANDING OFFICER

EXAMINED: RICHARD C. SHELL, LT, USNR U.S.N. NAVIGATOR

Figure 25. USS Acme Deck Log, June 16th, Page Two.

speeds while recovering Dan Buoy. 1900 commenced maneuvering to recover motor whaleboat. 1920 Recover motor whale boat. Recovered by divers from sunken PCF: Two brief cases, one body, unidentified. 2005 Away the motor whale boat. 2030 One buoy free from bottom. 2040 Recovered motor whaleboat. 2250 PCF alongside for transfer of parts. 2300 PCF away.

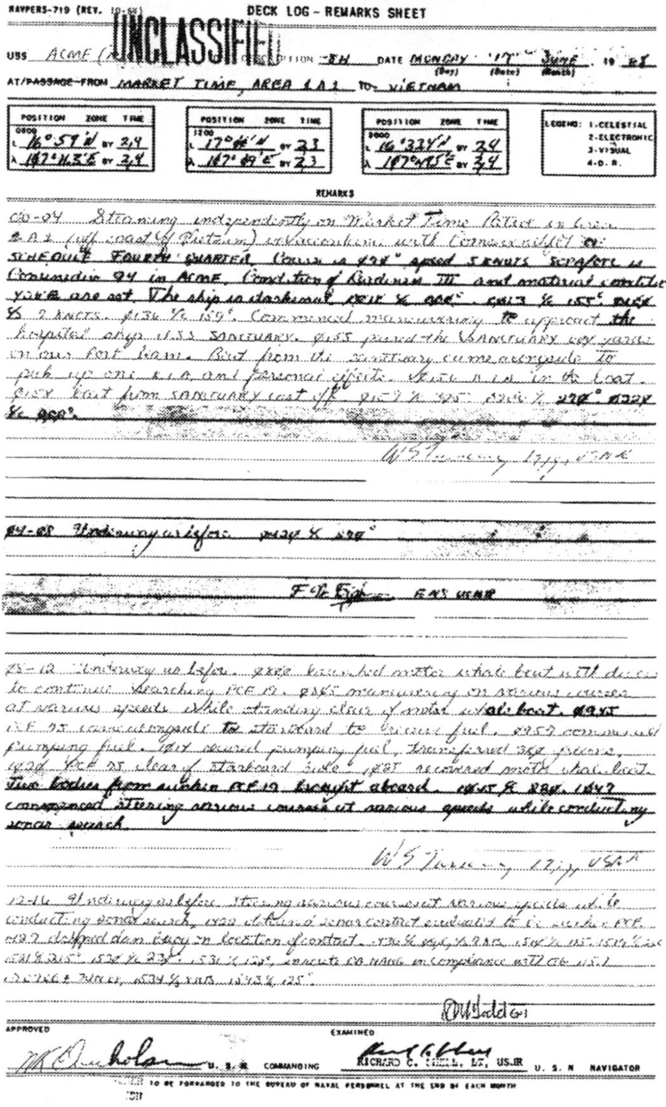

Figure 26. USS Acme Deck Log, June 17th, Page One

Larry Lail would take these remains after recording injuries and identification marks and place them in a body bag for transfer. Acme would proceed to seaward and south to rendezvous with USS Sanctuary. Reaching its location, a boat was sent from Sanctuary to pickup the remains of the first KIA of PCF-19 to be recovered. This took place at 0156 on June 17th. Larry would recall that this man had a tattoo of a deer's head on his forearm.

ANDEREGG, John Robert GMGSN, B51 99 83, USN

WOUNDED IN ACTION - 16 Jun 1968 on the SOUTH CHINA SEA
(COORDINATES YD 305795). Received
multiple shrapnel wounds both legs,
both arms and face with corneal
abrasion right eye and intra ocular
forign body left eye when PFC 19 on
routine patrol was sunk by enemy
artillery or rocket fire emanating
from land North Vietnam. Condition
and Prognosis Excellent

RESULT OF HOSTILE ACTION

BRTH   22 Apr 1948
NOK   ILL.
DUSTA NAVHOSP USS

HOSP

DAVIS, John D. LTJG USN 702453/1105

WOUNDED IN ACTION - 16 June 1968, SOUTH CHINA SEA.
Received head and scalp lacerations
shrapnel in leg from enemy while on
routine patrol in SOUTH CHINA SEA.
CONDITION SERIOUS PROGNOSIS FAIR

RESULT OF HOSTILE ACTION

BRTH 13 Apr 1942
NOK   Penna
DUSTA COMNAVSUPPACT SGN

DEPARTMENT OF THE NAVY

WASHINGTON. D.C. 20370

Larry Lail

The enclosed material is sent to you in response
to your request of 25 april 1996

Leigh R. War

NAVPERS 5216/21 (Rev. 8-61)

PERS 621D

Figure 27. Casualty reports on Davis and Anderegg.

Meanwhile, the condition of LTJG John Davis and GMGSN John Anderegg was released from their location aboard USS Repose (AH-16).

Larry Lail received this copy in 1996 in response to his request under the Freedom of Information Act. However, it turns out to be incorrect after speaking to John Davis. The injuries listed for Anderegg are his and the ones for him are for Anderegg. Notice that it lists them as wounded in action and result of hostile action. Both men were awarded Purple Hearts for this action.

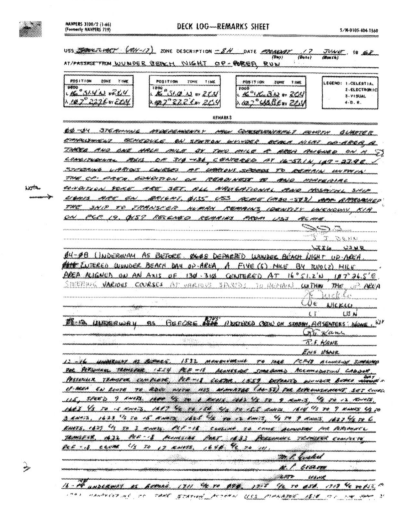

Figure 28. USS Sanctuary Deck Log, June 17th, Page One.

(Authors Note: This would be later identified as GMG2 Billy S. Armstrong from West Helena, Arkansas) The Deck Log of USS Sanctuary AH-17 for June 17th would reflect this transfer as follows:

0135 USS Acme (MSO-508) approached the ship to transfer human remains, identity unknown, KIA on PCF-19. 0157 Received remains from USS Acme.

Throughout the day, messages were sent up and down the chain of command as reports came in from commands near or at the scene. I show these in their original form with comments to show the confusion and even conflicting reports in reporting an incident of this magnitude. Notice that these messages previously Secret, have been declassified and released under the Freedom of Information Act.

The first one is from Commander Task Force 115 known as "Latch" and is sent to CINCPAC and other addressees. This is Captain Roy F. Hoffmann and he is in Cam Rahn Bay. The daytime group of these messages is Zulu time as are all message traffic around the world. The local times in the messages are referred to in Hotel time. This is because of the time zones around the world.

This message refers to the early reports of PCF-19 being sunk, two survivors rescued by Point Dume and medevaced to RDSMARDIV. This initial report believed the attack to have come from shore with rockets. PCF-12 shifted to Area 1A from Area C. PCF-12

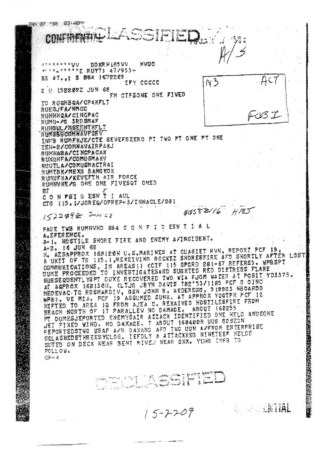

Figure 29. June 16th Message Traffic No. 3, Page One.

reports receiving hostile fire from beach north of 17th parallel. Point Dume reports enemy air attack from one helo and one jet fixed wing. About 0400H USS Boston reported two

USAF Aircraft Danang and two Unidentified Aircraft from USS Enterprise splashed three helos. Reportedly attacking nineteen helos sitting on deck near Ben Hai River near DMZ.

This early report is probably the most accurate being based on the first messages from the scene. This information was more than likely received by radio transmission using voice.

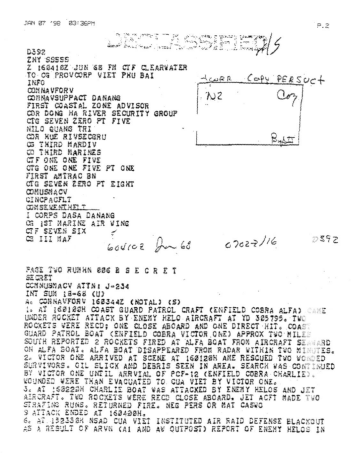

Figure 30. Message Traffic from Task Force Clearwater June 16th Page One.

The next message is from CTF Clearwater in Cua Viet to Coastal Group Province Corp Vietnam located at Phu Bai. It info's many other commands including COMUSMACV and COMSEVENTHFLT. This message describes the attack on Enfield Cobra Alpha, which is PCF-19. The message incorrectly describes it as a Coast Guard Patrol Craft.

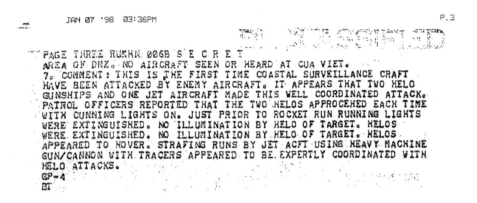

JAN 07 '98 03:36PM   P.3

PAGE THREE RUMHN 006B S E C R E T
AREA OF DMZ. NO AIRCRAFT SEEN OR HEARD AT CUA VIET.
7. COMMENT: THIS IS THE FIRST TIME COASTAL SURVEILLANCE CRAFT
HAVE BEEN ATTACKED BY ENEMY AIRCRAFT. IT APPEARS THAT TWO HELO
GUNSHIPS AND ONE JET AIRCRAFT MADE THIS WELL COORDINATED ATTACK.
PATROL OFFICERS REPORTED THAT THE TWO HELOS APPROCEHED EACH TIME
WITH CUNNING LIGHTS ON. JUST PRIOR TO ROCKET RUN RUNNING LIGHTS
WERE EXTINGUISHED. NO ILLUMINATION BY HELO OF TARGET. HELOS
WERE EXTINGUISHED. NO ILLUMINATION BY HELO OF TARGET. HELOS
APPEARED TO HOVER. STRAFING RUNS BY JET ACFT USING HEAVY MACHINE
GUN/CANNON WITH TRACERS APPEARED TO BE EXPERTLY COORDINATED WITH
HELO ATTACKS.
GP-4
BT

Figure 31. Message Traffic from Task Force Clearwater June 16th Page Two.

Later it describes the Coast Guard Patrol Boat Enfield Cobra Victor One as the rescue boat for the survivors. This is Point Dume. It explains the rocket attack on PCF-19 as by enemy helo aircraft and gives the location. Initial reports of one rocket close aboard and one direct hit were based on sightings not actual inspection of the sunken craft. At 0220H enemy helos and jet aircraft attacked Charlie boat. Two rockets were received close aboard. In fact there was only one rocket and it was seen coming from a hovering aircraft by the crew of PCF-12. The Charlie boat listed in this case is in fact PCF-12, which is now Enfield Cobra Alpha. PCF-69 had assumed Enfield Cobra Charlie and was much further south and was not attacked. The message describes the jet aircraft making two strafing runs, and return fire from PCF-12. This was not the case because the firing came from the hovering aircraft not the jets. PCF-12 crewmen saw a low altitude flyover by a fixed wing jet but it showed no lights and did not fire on PCF-12. Naval Support Activity Detachment Cua Viet instituted air raid defense blackout as a result of these reports by Alpha One and other DMZ outposts of enemy helos the area. No aircraft seen or heard at Cua Viet.

A message from III Marine Air Force COC or Chief of Staff details a daily summary of developments ending at 0900H on June 16th. It describes how reaction aircraft from the 366th TFW and USS Enterprise reported downing three enemy helicopters and sighting three others on Tiger Island.

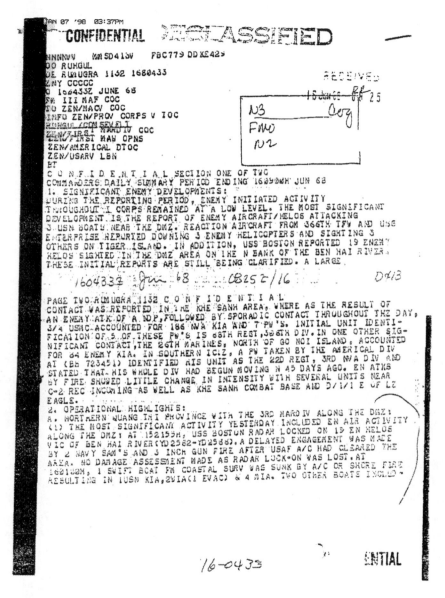

Figure 32. Message Traffic from III MAF Headquarters June 16th Page One.

In addition USS Boston reported 19 enemy helos sighted in the DMZ area on the bank of the Ben Hai River. These helos had been spotted earlier by the Marines along the DMZ as flying from the northern half of the DMZ in formation out to sea. Tiger Island is inside North Vietnamese waters and appeared to be supplied by helo and boat craft for some time. At 2155H, just before midnight on June 15th, Boston radar locked on 19 helos in the vicinity of the Ben Hai River.

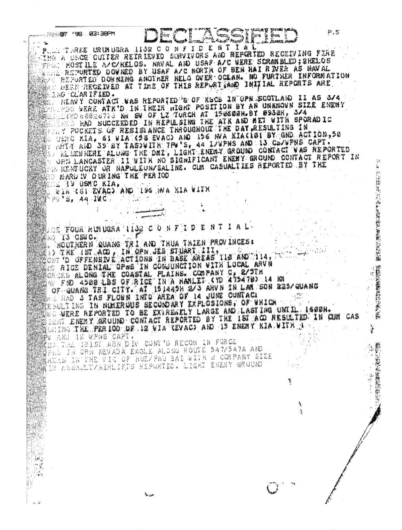

Figure 33. Message Traffic from III MAF Headquarters June 16th Page Two.

Two Navy SAM's made a delayed engagement and three-inch gunfire after USAF aircraft had cleared the area. At 0100H on June 16th, one Swift Boat was sunk by aircraft or shore fire resulting in one USN KIA, two WIA and four MIA. Two other boats, PT Dume and PCF-12 reported receiving fire from hostile aircraft/helos. Naval and USAF aircraft were scrambled: two helos were reported downed by USAF A/C north of Ben Hai River as Naval A/C reported downing another helo over the ocean.

By the end of June 16th, there had been much reported by the commands and forwarded up the Chain of Command. USS Acme had located the wreck of PCF-19 and retrieved one KIA, which was transferred to USS Sanctuary. The reports of downed helos by the USAF and Enterprise all occurred at night and there were no attacks during the day of June 16th. USS Acme crewman would observe frequent shelling by allied forces and bombing by aircraft into and north of the DMZ. No results were reported. This message from CTF-115 to CTG-115.1, info COMNAVFORV requests delay of destruction of PCF-19 for 24 hours. It asked for maximum effort to be exerted to locate any pieces of ordinance used in sinking of boat. As will be shown later, large pieces of missiles were found on Hobart and Boston on the strikes later that night, June 16/17th, just 24 hours after the hit on PCF-19. However, the divers found no pieces of ordinance on PCF-19. This message appears to have been sent to USS Acme. Acme was using the call sign of CTG One One Pt. One. It is not known whether or not this order was complied with.

A chart of the area shows the location of PCF-19 as found by USS Acme. It also shows the location of the Enfield Cobra Charlie patrol area.

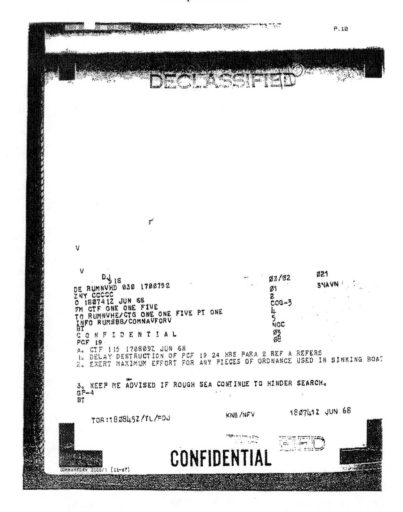

Figure 34. Message Traffic asking for delay in destruction of
PCF-19 to identify ordnance used.

Acme would return to the area on June 17th in the morning to continue the salvage operations, however, the helo incident was far from over as USAF Jets returned to the skies over the DMZ after midnight on June 16th/17th. It is important to keep these dates in perspective as the next evenings events unfolded. The Naval Ships moved back in to the DMZ area as night fell over the DMZ and Tiger Island area.

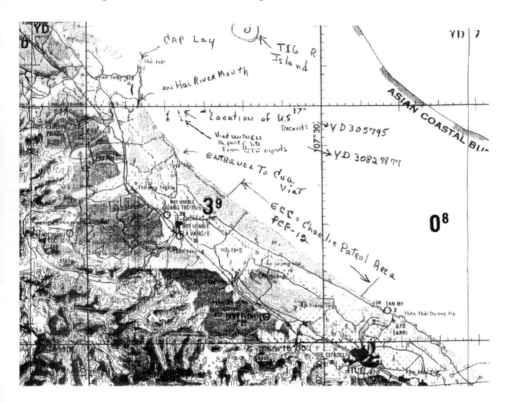

Figure 35. Chart showing locations of Tiger Island and the wreck of PCF-19.

CHAPTER TWELVE

June 17ᵗʰ, Friendly Fire Causes Death and Destruction

U SS Boston and USS Blandy with COMDESRON2 aboard steamed back into the
DMZ area during the day after trying to sort out the events of the previous
night. During the daytime hours there were flights of U.S. Jets strafing and bombing
the northern half of the DMZ and into North Vietnam itself as our forces kept the
enemy troops on the move. There were no reports of enemy helicopters flying or
sitting out in the open. Presumably they would be under camouflage or hidden
somewhere safe from the U.S. Aircraft and Navy Guns. Mike Stowe who was aboard
USS Boyd (DD-544) states that HMAS Hobart relieved them during the day. Hobart
was accompanied by USS Theodore Chandler (DD-717) and had moved down from
the vicinity of Dung Hoi to the area around Tiger Island. The four ships now prepared
for another night of action. RM3 Jim Fitch was aboard Theodore Chandler and he
related this report to me. I quote from Jim Fitch: We, Chandler, were DesRon 9 out of
Yokosuka. We were running Sea Dragon ops north of the DMZ with USS
Goldsborough, and then the Hobart relieved the Goldie. I believe we only ran one
mission (Dong Hoi?) when we were requested to move south and join up with a
cruiser (Boston or Chicago), (Authors Note: It was Boston and her shotgun USS
Blandy (DD-943). They had been involved in some kind of action near Tiger Island
the night before (same night PCF-19 got whacked). We moved south and set up a
picket line between Tiger Island and the mainland, stayed at General Quarters till
after midnight, no action so we were secured and they went to Condition Three. Had
not been in my rack (located directly beneath mount 52) long when we were awakened
by the mount firing before GQ went. They had picked up some kind of aircraft moving
toward the group. We had CAP but the area was so congested they sent the CAP out
of the area so we would not mistakenly shoot any friendlies. At some point several
missiles were fired (later identified as US manufacture). They were heat seekers and
homed in on the Hobart's stacks. Initially she was hit with a single missile, and then a little
later, two more impacted. What I saw in later message traffic they came from two USAF F-
105's coming back from a mission up north, supposedly they were fired at rotary wing
aircraft that the Chandler was engaged with, overshot and picked up the Hobart's signature.
I know our CIC guys said later that what the Hobart and us engaged was a large formation

of rotary wing aircraft. Initially, the Air Force denied they were involved, but the serial numbers off the missile parts found on the Hobart were traced to the airfield and the airframe they had been loaded on and the truth came out. There was a lot of confusion that night, but my take on it was that the two U.S. Air Force Jets and the rotary wing aircraft (NVA) were both pieces of the same incident. Unquote. Jim Fitch was an RM3 and sent this report to me by e-mail from Germany. Like many of the witnesses reporting on this incident, Jim has carried this story around in his memory all these years. It had such an impact on Jim and others that when they heard about this book, they readily supplied their facts to the case.

John Taylor, aboard USS Boston quotes a report in his diary from 1st Cav. Airmobility Developments, 1968, Chapter X Art 193, "Enemy Helicopters?" June 16th.

At 2055 hours a U.S. Radar Station reported that 10 unidentified helicopters had been located 6 km north of the Ben Hai River. During the remainder of the night of 16/17 numerous reports were received of enemy helicopters operating in the vicinity of the DMZ. Another report cited an attack on a US Navy boat by an unidentified aircraft. Finally, it was reported that many of the enemy helicopters were destroyed by USAF aircraft and by artillery (50cal"Dusters"). Two hours after the first report had been received, 7th AF dispatched a message stating that all aircraft, both helicopter and fixed-wing, operating in the I Corps Tactical Zone would be under the positive control of USAF ground radar stations. The USAF considered the helicopter sightings a serious threat to Danang Air Base and all other major installations in the I Corps Tactical Zone. As time passed and further investigations were conducted, it developed that no finite evidence was available to confirm that enemy helicopters had been observed in flight, on the ground, or in a damaged state following claims of destruction by friendly air. The previously accepted positive reports were discredited." Unquote.

Could it be that all these men were suffering from "mass hallucinations"? How could all of these reports from this area come in stating the same thing and then be discredited. Most of the time, forward observers reporting sightings of enemy movement do not generate this much activity. Although these sightings were reported all the way to MACV in Saigon, it became extremely difficult for these forward observers to believe they had been seeing things. Also, a U.S. Military that had been fighting a war for almost four years is suddenly told that they are victims of "bad communications", "faulty radar imaging" and "defective missiles". Missiles that destroyed enemy planes over North Vietnam, suddenly failed to track a target "locked on" and instead headed out to sea in search of a naval vessel. It is amazing that with all these "wild, and out of control" missiles flying around that none of the aircraft were hit. After all, these were "air to air" missiles. One would suppose that all these aircraft should have been grounded to find out the problem. Instead, the war went on as usual, only the witnesses were discredited to prevent embarrassment to the enemy.

John Taylor would continue with his account of the action aboard Boston just after midnight on June 16/17th. I quote from his report:

The gods must have been angry as that night, 16th and 17th Boston was attacked off the DMZ, south of Tiger Island, by USAF F-4D Phantoms from the 366th Tactical Fighter Wing (The Gunfighters) out of Danang. The 1950's Terrier SAM system is no match for Phantoms flying at over Mach One (850MPH). I was in Damage Control Central during GQ two nights ago when we picked up an incoming bogey approaching from the southeast 12,000 meters distant. We tried the coded IFF frequency, but no response. It's closing fast and the radarman is calling out the distance: 5,000 meters, 4,000 meters . . . PIRAZ (Positive Identification and Radar Advisory Zone) says no "friendlies" in the area, Danang says all their "birds" are accounted for. Well, this must be what it's like to be attacked by a MIG. The "hostile" knows we have locked on and makes a maneuver and our Terrier tracking loses him. Two missiles are fired which bracket the ship for and aft but miss. It's gone into the night. Close call. Next night, deja vu, bogey approaching, again not on the proper radio frequency, not identifying itself after numerous attempts to signal it. This time, "Whummmph!" the crunch of metal on metal, and silence. We're hit between the magazine and mount 52. As Assistant DCA, I take a party on deck and find pieces of a dud radar guided AIM-7 Sparrow III missile with "Raytheon Corp. Waltham, Mass." on them (same as the pieces found on Hobart). Luckily it's a dud. Out on deck, there are pieces of missile and bent metal.

I'm thinking:

1). The North Vietnamese have adapted ordnance from our downed planes to their MIGs.
2) Raytheon, Mass, that's a suburb of Boston, how ironic.
3). Next time we're not going to be so lucky since our air defenses are obsolete.

That night the HMAS Hobart (DDG-39) and USS Edson (DD-946) are also attacked nearby off Cap Lay. Hobart suffers two killed and five wounded. Boston took command of the two Sea Dragon and NGFS Units and steamed NE out of harms way to Yankee Station in the Gulf of Tonkin. It is the staging area for the 7th Fleet Carrier Task Group. Nearby is PIRAZ Station, where modern Belknap class guided missile frigates (DLG's) equipped with sophisticated Naval Tactical Data Systems (NTDS) in CIC vector all Navy, Marine, and USAF aircraft to and from their targets over North Vietnam and warn of any MIGs in the area. Since my arrival such PIRAZ alerts to Sea Dragon ships had become more common as more "hostiles" were making forays over land towards the South." Unquote.

Commenting on the above report, I have to say that it appears the IFF and other communications seem to be working over North Vietnam as Navy, and Air Force aircraft that must coordinate over the target fly these missions. Why did it all fall apart near the DMZ?

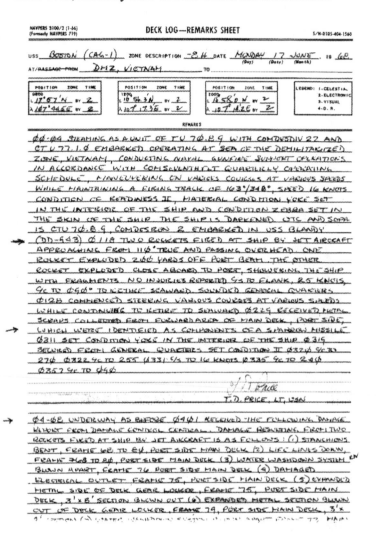

Figure 36. USS Boston Deck Log for June 17th. Page One

Notice that the deck log shows the two rockets (missiles) fired from jet aircraft as related by John Taylor came at 0118 on June 17th. That is just about 24 hours after PCF-19 was hit and sunk. It was very easy for the reports to lump the two attacks together in light of the publicity afforded Hobart and Boston on June 17th.

Message traffic for June 17th continues to add details. This one is from CTF-115 to CINCPACFLT and others.

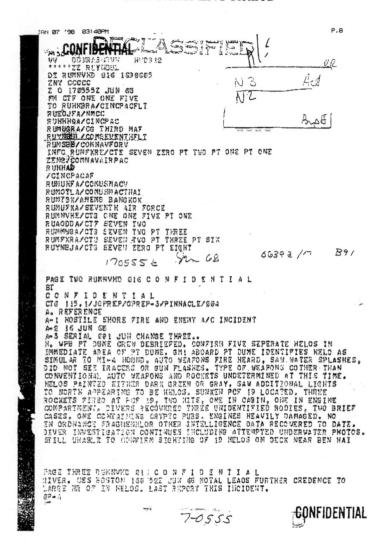

Figure 37. Message Traffic from CTF 115 to CINCPAC June 17th.

In this one, "The WPB Pt Dume crew was debriefed and confirmed five separate helos in immediate area of Pt Dume. GM1 aboard Pt. Dume identifies helo as similar to MI-4 Hound. Auto weapons fire heard, saw water splashes, and did not see tracers or gun flashes. Type of weapons other than conventional auto weapons and rockets undetermined at this time. Helos painted either dark green or gray saw additional lights to north appearing to be helos. Sunken PCF-19 is located, three rockets fired at PCF-19, two hits, one in cabin, one in engine compartment. Divers recovered three unidentified bodies, two brief cases. One contains crypto pubs. Engines heavily damaged. No EN ordnance fragments or other intelligence data recovered to date."

Here is more evidence of visual sightings by Point Dume who saw them close enough to get a description similar to my identification of this aircraft. Sorry, we were too busy to take photographs but this seemed to be the only proof the folks down south would believe.

The next message is a casualty report showing the four crewmen from PCF-19 and the bodies recovered, one on June 16th and two more on June 17th. At this time all four were listed as missing. The Vietnamese Liaison Petty Officer is not listed among the missing in this message; however, he is one of the bodies recovered on June 17th. His name was Bui Quang Thi. Message states that the bodies appear to be one Vietnamese, one Caucasian, and one Malayan and were transferred to USS Sanctuary.

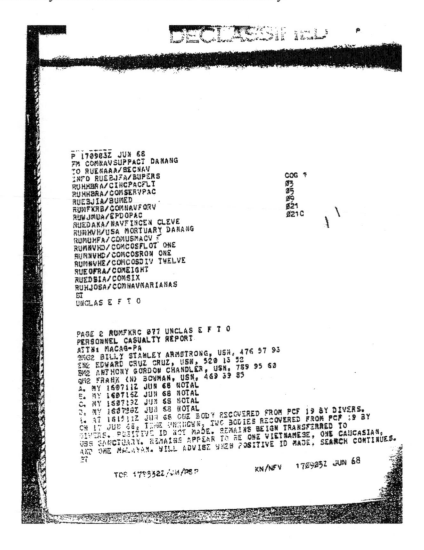

Figure 38. Message Traffic Listing PCF-19 Personnel Casualties.

The correct information is that only one body was transferred to a hospital ship, it was the USS Repose on June 16th. This body turned out to be GMG2 Stanley Armstrong from West Helena, Arkansas. He was 29 years old. The Vietnamese was Bui Quang Thi and the one listed as Malayan was EN2 Edward Cruz, 22 years old and he was from Inarajan, Guam. The last two bodies were retained on board Acme and delivered to Danang. Also listed on this message were BM2 Anthony Gordon Chandler, 23 years old from Warner Robbins, Georgia and QM2 Frank Bowman 32 years old from Walterboro, South Carolina.

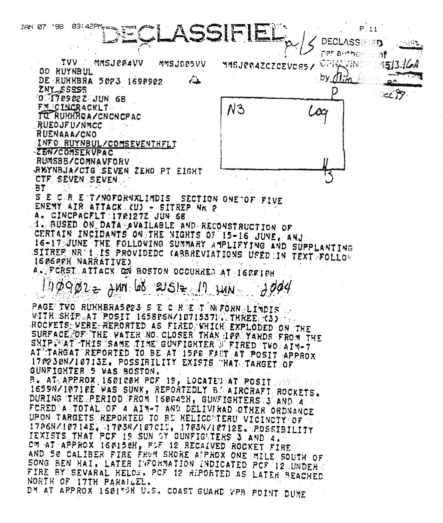

Figure 39. Message Traffic from CINCPACFLT to CNO, Page One.

This final message from June 17th is from CINPACFLT and states:

Based on data available and reconstruction of certain incidents on the nights of June 15-16, and 16-17 June, the following summary amplifying and supplanting SITREP 1 is provided. Abbreviations used in text follow 160600H narrative.

A. It explains how at 160010H three rockets were fired at USS Boston, which exploded no closer than 110 yards from the ship. At the same time Gunfighter 05 fired two AIM-7 missiles at a target. Possibility exists that this was Boston.

B. At approx 160100H aircraft rockets sank PCF-19 reportedly. During the period from 160042H, Gunfighters 03 and 04 fired a total of four AIM-7 missiles and delivered other ordnance upon targets reported to be helicopters in the nearby vicinity, (message details coordinates). Possibility exists that PCF-19 is sunk by Gunfighters 03 and 04. At approx 160150H, PCF-12 received rocket fire and 50-caliber fire from shore approx one mile south of Song Ben Hai. Later information indicated PCF-12 under fire by several helos. PCF-12 reported as later beached north of 17th Parallel. (Authors Note, PCF-12 was south of PCF-19 sinking position when she received the rocket and machine gunfire and it came from close range not from shore. Also PCF-12 never beached north of 17th parallel. Again these are early reports but they show the attempt to link the PCF-19 sinking and the PCF-12 attacks to Gunfighter aircraft by identifying their positions and the missiles fired. If this can be determined this accurately, how can they misidentify the target, helo vs a large Navy Cruiser?) At approximately 160156H U. S. Coast Guard WPB Point Dume was attacked by aircraft identified as one helo and one fixed wing jet. (Authors Note, This could have been one of our jets chasing and or attacking an enemy helo that was firing on Pt Dume. This possibility is not explored.)

C. At 170118H, four rockets were fired at Boston by a swept wing aircraft similar to F-4 or MIG. The first two appeared to fizzle out, third hit 100 yards close aboard. (Authors Note, This near miss caused extensive damage and pieces of an AIM-7 Sparrow missile were found on the deck 100 yards from the impact!!!! Imagine if one of these had hit PCF-19? Also imagine if one had passed between the radio antennae of PCF-12 and exploded close aboard? Well, the message tries to say that is exactly what happened. The crews of Pt Dume and PCF-12 and the divers on PCF-19 say a rocket did the damage and narrowly missed their boats. If the same missile that struck close to Boston had hit PCF-19 or near miss to PCF-12, where is the extensive damage to these boats)? At 170313H HMAS Hobart was attacked by two jet aircraft and returned fire with guns. Ship sustained hit by two rockets and reported holding rocket pieces of U.S. origin. Ship position vicinity Cap Lay. (Authors Note, This is two hours after Boston receives a near miss).

D. At 170331H USS Edson was attacked while in company with Hobart and Theodore Chandler. One rocket was fired which impacted in water with no damage. Firing aircraft identified by sound as jet aircraft. (Authors Note, The times of the attacks on Hobart and Edson are closely identified with the PCF-12 report of additional jet aircraft arriving from Danang from the south flying over Point Dume and PCF-12 asking for a flare to identify their locations).

E.   While the magnitude of enemy helicopter involvement in the subject incidents is not entirely discounted, lack of any intelligence indications tends to discredit numbers reported. Several factors tend to indicate that in some of the cases U.S.

Figure 40. Message Traffic from CINCPAC to CNO Page Two.

Forces made attacks. (Authors Note, Now this is a true statement and should have been left at that but the "spin" continues.) Correlation of Gunfighter aircraft attack times and places with positions and time of attacks on Boston (16 June) and PCF-19, and identification of U.S. missile fragments resulting from attacks on Boston (17 June) and Hobart offer strong indication that these attacks were in fact not enemy. (Authors Note, Whether intentional or not, this statement lumps the two events together and blames the U.S. aircraft based on the missile fragments found the next night June 17th.) Also, there is no conclusive evidence to indicate the presence of NVA fixed wing aircraft in the DMZ during the action of 15-17 June. (Authors Note: The sightings of "fixed wing" aircraft stated that they were "swept wing aircraft" similar to F-4 or MIG's. Since the helos were assumed to be hostile, the silhouette of a swept wing aircraft could be seen as MIG type aircraft.) There are no reports of friendly helo losses, nor is their any known debris recovered to substantiate shoot down of NVA helos. (Authors Note, There were no underwater searches for wreckage undertaken nor were there any known reconnaissance flights over Tiger Island reported to assess ground damage. The U.S. jet aircraft were sent to the DMZ to attack "something" and these targets were reported to "hover" and move slowly similar to helos. The resulting attacks caused the damage to the Navy ships. It is not enough to say that because no debris was found that the helos did not exist. The fact that no friendly helo losses were reported should indicate that the "hovering" aircraft had to be enemy. Did they appear to be moving south in a threatening manner, probably not? I still believe that some kind of swimmer operation was in progress and PCF-19 stumbled on to it. PCF-12 and Pt Dume's encounters with the "hovering aircraft" could have been part of this same operation. The helo attacks appeared to be defensive in nature attacking PCF-12 when she approached the two helos). The message continues with the summary of personnel casualties, material damage and aircraft ordnance expenditures. Note that at this time the casualties to PCF-19 are listed as 3 KIA, 2 MIA, and 2 WIA. (Authors Note: The PCF-19 KIA's were later identified as Cruz, Armstrong, and Bui Quang Thi. The MIA's were Chandler and Bowman. The WIA's were Davis and Anderegg). Further notes state that F-4's were launched in response to Dong Ha having visual sighting of ten helos, one contact on radar. Helos active vicinity DMZ. This was at 152030H, helos taken under fire by Marine artillery. If strikes were successful photo aircraft would be sent. Two Misty aircraft (assume these are photo recon aircraft) conducted visual recon area Ben Hai River mouth to 8KM inland, Tiger Island and other possible heliport sites. (CTG 77.0 170138Z) refers. I do not have that message. At 152139H Dong Ha direct air support center advised Waterboy that four unidentified choppers were proceeding from the mouth of the Ben Hai River to Tiger Island at 120 knots at 800 to 1000 feet. Dong Ha information source was 12th Marine Brigade. At 2140H Action taken to identify the reported choppers. MACSOG Operations confirmed that they had no choppers in the area. (Authors Note, These are the "spooks" that might have been operating there) CUS confirmed they had no choppers in the area. DASC, Direct Air Support Center Victor confirmed with 1ˢᵗ Cav and 101ˢᵗ Airborne that they had no choppers airborne. Navy Liaison was called and asked to confirm that the Navy had no choppers or slow movers in the area.

JAN 07 '98 03:44PM   P.13/

DECLASSIFIED

```
PAGE FIVE RUHHBRA   123 S E C R E T NOFORN LIMDIS
(2) MATERIAL DAMAGE:
A. PCF 719 SUNK.
B. BOSTON 7 SPS-30 DAMAGED, OTHER MINOR DMG.
C. HOBART - SPS-40 RUDUR DAMAGED, MISSILE SYSTEM
DAMAGED, MOUNT 52 DUMAGED.
(3) ALLIED SHIPS RAPORTED RECEIVING 15 ROUNDS
OF ROCKAT FIRE. AIRCRAFT RAPORTED EXPENDING 12 AIM-7.
(4) SHIPS ATTACKED (NUMBER OF TIMES):
A. BOSTON (2)
B. PCF-19 (1)
C. POINT DUME (1)
D. HOBART (1)
E. PCF-12 (1)
F. EDSON (1)
12  2    .26-5GFIM
                         GMT 1571 JUF VEC
IHVNNL1 2030H REPORT RECAIVED FROM DONG HA UNIDENT AIRBORNE
HELOS ACTIVE VICINITY DMZ. VISUAL SIGHTING
INCLUDES TEN HELOS, 1 CONTACT HELD ON RADAR.
POSIT 351714 FROM CH JAPO (DONG HA TACANLM
HELOS TAKEN UNDER FIRE BY MARINE ARTY. FOPWX


PAGE SIX RUHHBRA5023 S E C R E T NOFORN LIMDIS
F4'S LAUNCHED FOR STRIKE. ALERT RECCE A/C
WILL PHOTO BDA IF STRIKES SUCCESSFUL. TWO
MISTY A/C CONDUCTED VISUAL RECCE AREA BEN HAI
RIVER MOUTH TO 8 KM INLAND, TIGER ISLAND ANJ
OTHER POSSIBLE HELIPORT SITES. (CTG 77.P
170138Z).
152139H   DONG HA DIRECT AIR SUPPORT CENTER (DASC)
ADVISED WATERBOY THAT FOUR (4) UNCDENTIFIED CHOPPERS WERE
PROCEEDING FROM THE MOUTH OF THE BEN HAI RIVER TO
TIGER ISLAND AT 120 KNOTS AT 800 TO 1000 FEET.
DONG HA DASC INFORMATION SOURCE WAS 12TH MARINE
BRIGADE. (AFSSO SEVENTH AF 160445Z).                    5
152140H ACTION TAKEN TO IDANTIFO THE REPORTED CHOPPERS.
MACSOG OPERATIONS CONFIRMED THAT THEY HAD NO
CHOPPERS IN THE AREA. CUS CONFORMED THAEY HUD NO
CHOPPERU IN THE AREA. DASC VICTOK CONFIRMED WITH
1ST CAV AND 101ST ABN THAT THEY HUD NO CHOPPERS AIR-
BOARNE. NAVY LIAISON WAS CULLED AND ASKAD TO CONFIRM
THAT THE NAVY HAD NO CHOPPERS OR SLOET
SE L
ETSW MOVERS IN THE
BT
```

DECLASSIFIED

Figure 41. Message Traffic from CINCPAC to CNO Page Three.

F.   (Authors Note: As noted above, there was "much communication" going on to identify these helos and communication between the services was coordinated. As the final inquiry results would state however, it was a confused, disorganized, multi-unit screw up resulting in friendly casualties).

UNITED KINGDOM
Air Force: 38 × Boeing Vertol Chinook HC 1, 43 × Aérospatiale SA 341, 43 × SA 330E, 19 × Westland Sea King HAR 3, 15 × Wessex HC 2, 2 × Wessex Mk 4, 8 × Wessex Mk 5
Army: 9 × Aérospatiale SE 313B, 4 × Agusta A 109, 182 × Aérospatiale SA 341, 104 × Westland Lynx AH 1, (+ 5) × Lynx Mk 7, 98 × Scout
Navy: 31 × Aérospatiale SA 341, 45 × Westland Lynx HAS 2, 33 (+ 7) × Lynx Mk 3, 77 (+ 5) × Sea King HAS 2/5, 10 × Sea King AEW Mk 2, 24 (+ 10) × Sea King HC 4, 36 × Wasp, 18 × Wessex 5
Marines: 12 × Aérospatiale SA 341B, 6 × Westland Lynx AH 1

UNITED STATES OF AMERICA
Air Force: 25 × Bell TH-1F, 120 × UH-1F, 18 × UH-1N, 59 × HH-1N, 22 × HH-1H, 2 × AH-1G, (+ 80) × Bell-Boeing CV-22A, 6 × Boeing Vertol CH-46B, 6 × CH-47A, 12 × CH-47C, 35 × Sikorsky HH-3E, 29 × HH-53B/C, 10 × HH-3F, 18 × CH-3E, 9 × HH-53H, 10 × UH-60A, 1 × HH-60A
Army: 334 × Bell UH-1, 10 × EH-1H, 220 × UH-1V, 1828 × OH-58A/C, 16 (+ 100) × OH-58D, 86 × AH-1G, 193 × AH-1S, 10 × TH-1S, 126 (+ 23) × Modernised AH-1S, 407 × Mod AH-1S, 124 × Boeing Vertol CH-47, 106 × CH-47B, 265 × CH-47C, 113 (+ 215) × CH-47D, 348 × McDD (Hughes) OH-6A, 240 × TH-55A, 50 (+ 625) × AH-64A, 685 (+ 363) × Sikorsky UH-60A, 72 × CH-54, (+ 40) × EH-60A
Coast Guard: 22 (+ 74) × Aérospatiale SA 366G, 60 × Sikorsky HH-52A, 36 × HH-3F
Marine Corps: 200 × Bell UH-1E, 20 × TH-1E, 50 × TH-1L, 170 × UH-1N, 8 × VH-1N, 56 × AH-1J, 49 × AH-1T, (+ 42) × AH-1W, (+ 552) × Bell-Boeing MV-22A, 18 × Boeing Vertol CH-46A, 43 × CH-46D, 267 × CH-46E/F, 99 × Sikorsky CH-53A/D, 18 × VH-53D, 82 (+ 15) × CH-53E, (+ 9) × VH-60E
Navy: 27 × Bell UH-1E, 27 × TH-1K, 32 × TH-57A, 49 × TH-57B, 89 × TH-57C, (+ 50) × Bell-Boeing HV-22A, 46 × Boeing Vertol HH-46A, 19 × UH-46A, 12 × UH-46D, 127 (+ 36) × Kaman SH-2F, 12 × Sikorsky VH-3E, 96 × SH-3G, 109 × SH-3H, 12 (+ 24) × CH-53E, (+ 32) × MH-53E, 15 × RH-53A, 23 × RH-53D, 52 (+ 156) × SH-60B, (+ 76) × SH-60F

URUGUAY
Air Force: 5 × Bell UH-1B, 4 × UH-1H, 2 × 222
Navy: 4 × Bell 47G-2, 1 × 222A, 2 × Sikorsky CH-34

VENDA
Air Force: 1 × Aérospatiale SA 316B, 1 × MBB-Kawasaki BK 117

VENEZUELA
Air Force: 4 × Aérospatiale SE 3160, 8 × Agusta A 109, 4 × Agusta-Sikorsky S-61R, 14 × Bell UH-1B D H, 2 × UH-1N, 7 × 206L-1, 2 × 212, 2 × 214ST, 2 × 412
Army: 12 × Aérospatiale SA 316B, (+ 6) × Agusta A 109, 2 × Agusta-Sikorsky AS-61, 12 × Bell UH-1H, 2 × 205A, 3 × 206B
Navy: 12 × Agusta-Bell AB 212AS, 2 × Bell 47G

VIETNAM
Air Force: 4 × Bell UH-1D/H, 10 × Boeing Vertol CH-47A, 30 × Mil Mi-4, 10 × Mi-6, 60 × Mi-8, 30 × Mi-24D
Navy: 17 × Kamov Ka-25A, 10 × Mil Mi-4

YEMEN (NORTH)
Air Force: 2 × Aérospatiale SA 316B, 2 × Agusta-Bell AB 204, 6 × AB 206, 6 × AB 212, 2 × Mil Mi-4, 12 × Mi-8

YEMEN (SOUTH)
3 × Mil Mi-4, 8 × Mi-8, 12 × Mi-24

YUGOSLAVIA
Air Force: 15 × Aérospatiale SE 3160, 3 × SA 341G, 17 × SA 341H, 2 × Agusta A 109, 5 × Agusta-Bell AB 205, 2 × AB 212, 10 × Mil Mi-4, 29 × Mi-8, 110 (+ 22) × Soko-Aérospatiale SA 341H, 10 × Soko-Westland Whirlwind Srs 2

ZAIRE
Air Force: 4 × Aérospatiale SE 3160, 3 × SA 316B, SA 321J, 11 × SA 330, 1 × AS 332L, 7 × Bell 47G

ZAMBIA
Air Force: 5 × Aérospatiale SE 313B, 8 × SA 316B, 16 × Agusta-Bell AB 47G-4A, 20 × AB 205A, 3 × AB 206, 2 × Bell 212, 11 × Mil Mi-8

ZIMBABWE
Air Force: 3 × Aérospatiale SE 3160, 10 × SA 316B (+ 30 stored), 8 × Agusta-Bell AB 205, 2 × AB 412, (+ 10) × AB 412 Griffon

Source
" World Military Helecopters" by Elfan ap Rees
Published in 1986 by Jane's Publishing Company Limited

192

Figure 42. Page from World Military Helicopters"
Listing Aircraft belonging to North Vietnam in 1968.

A copy of a page from a book titled "World Military Helicopters" by Elfan ap Rees published in 1986 by Jane's Publishing Company Limited, shows the number of helos belonging to North Vietnam: Note that the Air Force had 30 Mi-4 and 10 Mi-6 and 60 Mi-8 Helos. The Navy had 10 Mi-4 helos. These all came from the Russians. Where these helos were located in June 1968 is not certain but aircraft similar to these were flying from the mainland north of the Ben Hai River to Tiger Island. This many witnesses cannot be wrong.

As dawn broke over the DMZ area, Hobart and her escorts, Boston, Edson, Theodore Chandler, and Blandy had moved closer to the Carrier Task force to assess the damage of the previous night. Hobart would proceed to Subic Bay for repairs and return to the gun line seeing much more action in the war.

RADM S.H. Moore, COMCRUDESDIV 7th FLT begins Navy Investigation. Later, CINCPACFLT ADM U.S. Grant Sharp and COMSEVENTHFLT VADM W.F. Bringle fly to Subic Bay to offer formal condolences to the Hobart and order investigation to be upgraded to the Joint Services level.

During the day of June 17th, the rescue/salvage operation of PCF-19 would continue as Acme moved back into position near the wreck close to the beach and just south of the Ben Hai River.

CHAPTER THIRTEEN

June 17th
Rescue and Salvage of PCF-19 Continues,
Investigation Begins

U SS Acme returned to the site of the sinking of PCF-19. The special sonar was activated again as she approached the anchorage of June 16th. The sonar screen lit up with a contact on the bottom and the motor whaleboat crew prepared to launch. Suddenly, the bridge called out, "Hold on, this doesn't look right." Further examination between the bridge watch checking landmarks and the sonar plot revealed that this "contact" was not PCF-19. It was a "hard contact" but the location was not correct. Acme moved in closer to shore and located the wreck of PCF-19 once again. (Authors Note: I wonder, as have others, if this first contact could have been the enemy helo believed to have been shot down by the PCF-12 forward gunner, Tom Klemash.) Unfortunately, Acme did not return to the first sighting with divers to investigate the contact on this mostly clear bottom. Once in position, at 0800, the motor whaleboat was launched with divers to continue the search of the PCF-19. While standing clear of the motor whaleboat, Acme received Enfield Cobra Alpha alongside to receive fuel and then used her services to ferry one of the crewman to Cua Viet. PCF-75 had relieved PCF-101 as Enfield Cobra Alpha earlier in the morning and would stand by to assist Acme as the salvage continued. Keeping the sampans clear of the area was also the mission of PCF-75.

The crew of the Acme motor whaleboat included the coxswain, Dave Campbell, SN, 19 years old from Mesa, Arizona. The engineer was an engineman named Tom Doble, from Virginia. He now lives in Manasas, Virginia. Both of these men have given me statements detailing the experience aboard the motor whaleboat during the recovery operations.

I do not have a copy of the divers report; it has been impossible to find in the Naval Archives.

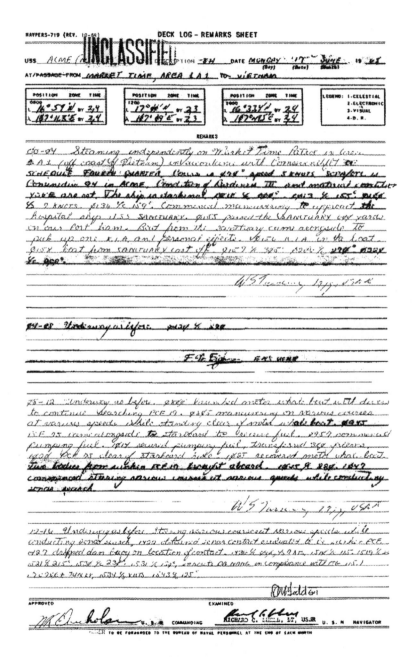

Figure 43. USS Acme Deck Log June 17th Page One.

Figure 44. USS ACME (MSO-508)

USS Acme, shown above is a wooden hulled minesweeper and carried sophisticated sonar called a Variable Depth Sonar (VDS). According to Dave Campbell there was actually a hole in the ship to accommodate the sonar that was retracted upward and into the forward berthing compartment. When lifted into the compartment it really smelled bad from the seawater.

NHA-BE   VieT NAM April 1967

Figure 45. Dave Campbell, coxswain of the MWB.

Dave Campbell is shown in the above pictures and I quote excerpts from his report to me on the salvage operation. "Quote"

This special sonar enabled Acme to locate the sunken Swift Boat easily. Being that close to North Vietnam, the Acme wanted to get the job done quickly.

We were in the Danang area when we received the message to proceed to the DMZ, it was on a Sunday as I recall. The first body brought aboard the motor whaleboat was GMG2 Armstrong according to the waistband on his jockey skivvies. When I put his body in the body bag, the motor whaleboat was tossing and pitching badly and it was very hot. I tried to get as much water out of the bag as possible because it was too heavy. This was the first body found on the afternoon of June 16th. It came from the forward berthing area. When trying to board Acme it was rolling heavily which caused the motor whaleboat to bang against the ship. As I tried to get Armstrong's body bag out of the boat and on to the ship, some water and I thought blood leaked out of the bag and hit me in the face. I still remember that feeling and it made me sick. I sucked it up and continued to lift the body onto the deck and carried it to the fantail. This is a lot for a 19-year-old kid from Arizona to absorb. Doc Lail helped me and then sent me below to take a shower. I felt bad for Armstrong at the time and was hoping and praying that he didn't suffer. Acme got underway shortly thereafter and went out to meet the hospital ship where Armstrong's body was transferred.

The next day we returned to the site and continued the operation. It was hot as hell again and we were about 1,000 to 1,500 meters from the beach. The seas were rough sometimes 2-3 ft swells and choppy. The Acme set off to the southeast about 500 meters from us. The divers with about a 30-foot line tied us to the PCF-19. I could actually see the boat between the swells. I am sure you know that as the swell ebbs, we go down. I could actually see the American Flag on the boat. It was sure heartbreaking. The water was pristine, however a small trail of oil was evident about 10 meters to the southeast of us. The tide (I think) was southbound during the recovery.

There was some kind of shelling going on to the west of us, maybe 3-10 miles. We could hear and see the shells. We thought it was a battleship (New Jersey)? (Authors Note: USS New Jersey did not arrive on station until September. Dave must have seen the USS Boston, which is a heavy cruiser.) Also saw a small helo and a piper type plane, probably Forward Air Controller. The Acme had to have a lot of help and since we only had 50 calibers and a single 40mm on board, she could not adequately defend herself. To this day I wonder why we didn't have any more coverage (help) from PCF's or any other boats. We worried about getting our butts shot off being so close to the beach. We took some sporadic small arms fire close to sunset on the first day. The waterspouts were evident, but seemed unintentional or just fell there. I suppose they were from a ways off. The ship was not aware of our (whaleboat) concern. Divers didn't know, we had no radio, and the boat crew didn't have any weapons at all. I guess it didn't matter anyway. It was still very hot!! I guess the FAC took care of it because we got out OK. If I recall we spent three days working there.

One of the divers brought up a handgun. It was a beautiful revolver, I remember asking one of the divers if I could have it. I was of course turned down.

I also recall putting the bodies on the starboard fantail of the Acme and recommending we place a two and a half inch fire hose feeding a seawater spray to keep the body bags cool. It didn't help much because it was so hot.

Dave Campbell "Unquote"

Tom Doble was the engineer of the Acme motor whaleboat and when I contacted him he had to really think to remember the details after 37 years. He did his best however and his statement follows. "Quote"

What do I remember? by Tom Doble.

I have been pondering that question ever since you called the other day. Trying to put together what really happened and what I imagine happened. Thirty-seven years is a long time especially when you try to forget or at least try not to remember and there is a difference, at least in my mind. OK here I go, as I picture it we, the USS Acme, were in a cove about 1,000 meters from the beach. Jets were coming over strafing the beach while we were preparing to launch the motor whaleboat for one of the three trips to the dive site. The first trip (this would be June 16th) we recovered one body and this I am a little foggy about. After we returned to the Acme I, as usual, went to the after engine room to stand watch. I know nothing about the hospital ship. (Authors Note: Since Tom was an engineer and below decks most of the time underway, he would not be aware of the ship's movements alongside or transfer of remains to the ship unless someone told him. I was an engineer and a lot happens when you are in the world of engine rooms and boiler rooms that do not impact you.) After my watch we were back on site (hot zone). Some of us were on the fantail. The fantail was pointing north; at least to the best of my recollection, there was a lot of action. Here again it seems like I remember this but I could just be imagining it. I think there was some kind of night action as long as we were up there. The second day we pulled up two bodies, (this would be June 17th) and that is when one of the divers brought up the revolver. I can't remember if a ship from Danang came up that night and got those bodies or not. I think they did. (Authors Note: Actually the Acme steamed down to Danang that night to deliver the bodies to the hospital.) That afternoon we got another body, last body. All three were placed under the water hose on the fantail. (Note: This makes a total of four bodies recovered.) Well that's the best I can remember. I saw the boat on sonar and the nose was down slightly, maybe 8, 10, or 15 degrees, not much. I got a lump in my stomach knowing I would be part of a group that would be pulling up some of our guys who gave it all. It's still hard for me to think about after all these years.

BAD FEELING

The cove. The best way I can describe it would be like a horseshoe. (Authors Note: Not a big issue except for Tom and Larry Lail's recollection of a cove or land on three sides of the area they were searching for PCF-19 in. The charts do not show a cove except farther north into North Vietnam, several miles from the site identified in official records. The divers describe a cove like view of the shoreline with land extending away to three sides and hills behind the beach. From the perspective of the water it appeared as a cove. The Marines would see a different view, however as their position on land looking to seaward would be different. On the chart below you can see the outline of the shore. The terrain gradually rises until the hills rise out of the sand dunes and up to the base of the mountains. It is not a matter of where the PCF-19 is located that is in question here instead the view of the terrain from Acme or the shore by the Marines.)

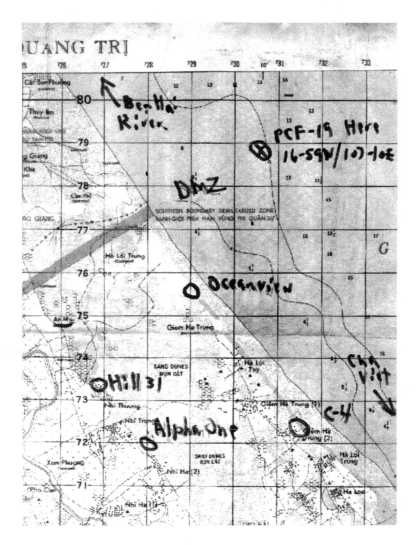

Figure 46. Chart Showing the Terrain Near the DMZ.

Note the seemingly unbroken shoreline for this area, which were mostly sand dunes and salt marshes. The Marines describe it as like a desert with an ocean view.)

The jets pounded the beach and I mean pounded. You could see sh__ being blown everywhere. It was a show sitting out in the whaleboat.

This is pretty much how I remember it. I hope it helped and THE BOAT WAS NO MORE THAN A THOUSAND METERS OFF THE BEACH.

This is the truth to the best of my recollection.

Thomas I. Doble. Unquote.

Here you see two accounts from the boat crew of Acme used in the salvage. It is a very real and I am certain stark memory for two young sailors on a ship not normally involved in heavy combat. They are both to be commended and it is another example of witnesses carrying this memory around for all these years not knowing the rest of the picture.

The divers reported that the inside of the PCF was very chaotic with mattresses, clothing and other debris floating around inside. The two bodies found were EN2 Cruz from the forward cabin area and BM2 Chandler from the pilothouse. The revolver recovered by the divers belonged to Chandler. The motor whaleboat would return to the wreck and retrieve one more body in the afternoon and it would be placed on deck with the other two. It turned out to be Bui Quang Thi, the SVNN interpreter. As darkness fell, Acme proceeded to Danang where she anchored for the night. HM1 Larry Lail had prepared the documents for the remains noting all tattoos and body characteristics for the records. He did not know at this time which remains were which and did not learn their names until 1995 when he and I found each other. It was just one of many ghosts that haunted this hospital corpsman aboard a small minesweeper pressed into special duty.

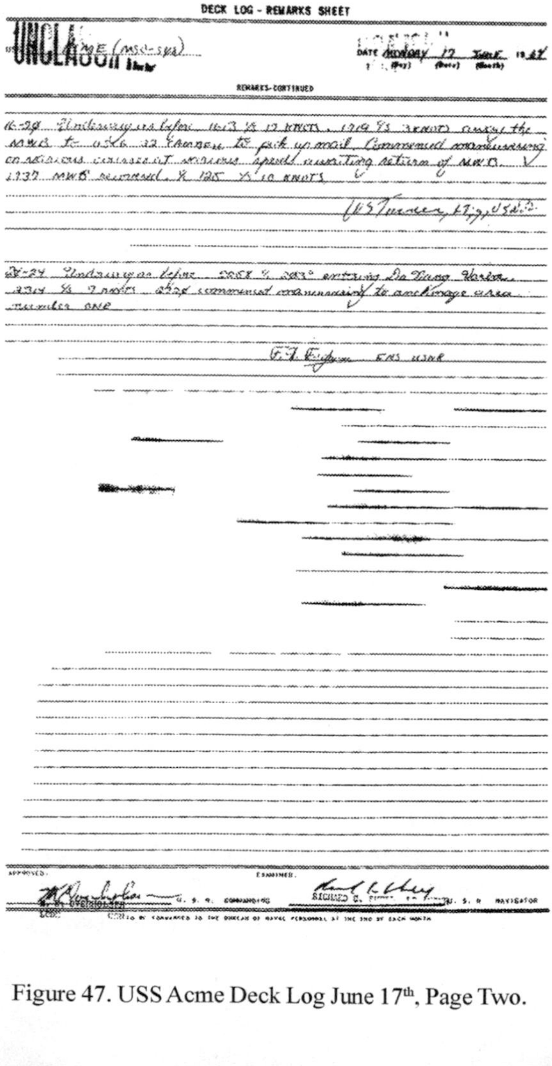
DECK LOG - REMARKS SHEET

UNCLA... (MSO-508)

DATE Monday 17 June 1967

REMARKS-CONTINUED

16-20 Underway as before ... 12 knots ... pick up mail. Commenced maneuvering on various courses at various speeds awaiting return of MWB.
1937 MWB secured ... 10 knots

20-24 Underway as before ... entering Da Nang Harbor. ... commenced maneuvering to anchorage area number one

ENS USNR

APPROVED: U.S.N. COMMANDING EXAMINED: U.S.N. NAVIGATOR

Figure 47. USS Acme Deck Log June 17th, Page Two.

Page two of June 17th Deck log for Acme shows her underway for Danang at 1737 at 10 knots.

Up at the DMZ the war returned that night after a noisy but fairly calm day close to the beach for the crew of Acme.

Acme would finish their mission on June 17th and after sending the divers ashore at Cua Viet, proceed to Danang with three bodies on board plus the remains of Armstrong which was delivered to Sanctuary on June 16th, makes a total of four KIA's recovered. The bodies were in body bags and placed together on the fantail of Acme. The cooling was provided, using water from a fire hose spraying on the bodies. Under the watchful eye of the deck crew, the three bodies of the PCF-19 crewmen lay waiting transfer to Danang and ultimately home. Two men rescued by Point Dume and one MIA, QM2 Frank Bowman whose body floated away from the raft when he died after the boat had sunk. The body was never found.

Acme returned to its anchorage in the harbor. It is not known exactly what happened after the transfer but the remains of Bui Quang Thi would be released to the South Vietnamese Navy and the two crewmen later identified as EN2 Edward Cruz and BM2 Anthony Chandler would be moved to "C" Med at the Hospital in Danang. "C" Med is similar to a M.A.S.H. Unit and is the intake unit for all KIA casualties.

The Marines would have another busy night of June 17/18th. From the monthly summary, the following reports describe the action. The first ones would be after midnight of June 17th.

Elements Co "A" at Oceanview, observed 12 NVA, fully equipped and armed moving north, vicinity YD 286746. Called 105MM arty mission with unknown results.

Two Xenon lights depart CP enroute to Oceanview. (Authors Note: Here is the beginning of an amazing story related to me by Major Richard Lennon of 1st Amtracs. A tank was sent up to Oceanview with a Xenon light mounted on its turret. It was to be buried in the sand during the day and uncovered in nighttime to be used in getting a visual of the UFO/helicopters. Accompanied by several visitors (VIP's) and the French AP photographer, Henri Huet, this mission under Major Lennon took place over several nights. It was never able to illuminate the helicopters from the distance as they did not approach Oceanview close enough to see them and they still remained hidden during the day. There were reports from USS Blandy and Boston of seeing the helicopters sitting on the ground at Tiger Island but these were not confirmed. I am certain the reconnaissance aircraft must have photographed them because the air strikes during the day and night were looking for this target. Some of the Marines found themselves victims of press jokes because no one believed the UFO/helicopter story. Those that stuck by their story were sent to Quang Tri and debriefed. Only after they recanted their story did they return to their units along the DMZ. Henri Huet took a picture at Oceanview of a sign that said "Chief Chopper Spotters". That photo, which appeared in some newspapers back home, was destroyed years later. Major Lennon has written to AP on a number of occasions, but they cannot locate the negative any longer.)

Elements "A" Troop, 3/5 Cav, USA, observed one VC guiding five NVA armed with AK-47's and a machine gun. Took them under fire, wounded and captured one VC. Check of area revealed two blood trails.

Tower, at Amtrac CP, reports two UFO's at 2 o'clock, 8000 meters.

Co "A", at C-4 position, reports two UFO's due east of C-4 position.

Elements Co "A", at Oceanview, reports six UFO's, vicinity the mouth of the Ben Hai River.

Tower, at Amtrac CP, reported UFO flying north over the peninsula.

Medivac of VC POW wounded in firefight by "A" Troop, 3/5 Cav, USA was completed.

Tower, at Amtrac CP, reports one UFO moving north from Tiger Island at a high rate of speed. (Authors Note: Since these sightings were visual or using a night observation device and were lighted aircraft, some of these could have been U.S. Jets on missions either following or attacking the helos. UFO simply means the originator does not know the identity of the aircraft.)

Tower, at Amtrac CP, reports two UFO's on azimuth of 5370 mils at a distance of 10,000 meters.

Co "A" at Oceanview, using PPS-5 radar, detected seven personnel moving southwest, vicinity YD 298716. Fired 81 MM mortar mission with unknown results.

Co "A" at Oceanview reports UFO being fired on in vicinity of C-2 position. (Note: This could be Gio Linh, one of the Marine outposts.)

The Marines continued to report and even fire on UFO's through June 18th according to this report. Boston deck logs for Wednesday June 19th show them operating approximately 30 miles off Cap Lay, which is the large peninsula north of the DMZ also known as Point Betty. During this time period Boston maneuvers at various speeds and courses moving in closer to shore when called on to deliver Naval Gunfire Support and to hit targets of opportunity in the north half of the DMZ. Boston is steaming independently as a unit of Task Unit 70.8.9 with COMDESDIV 22 and Commander Task Unit 77.1.0 embarked.

The war continues unabated throughout South Vietnam and with the rescue/salvage and final destruction of PCF-19 by the divers. USS Acme returned to its Market Time Mission. For the remains of the PCF-19 crew, their processing has begun. For the survivors of PCF-19 on board USS Repose, LTJG John Davis and GMGSN John Anderegg would begin their slow recovery from their wounds. The physical wounds would heal but the mental wounds caused by this night of terror would not heal for many years, if ever. Coupled with a finding of "friendly fire", these wounds became guilt and wonder as to why it happened and why they survived when others did not. For the crews of PCF-12, USCG Point Dume, NGLO Ltjg Pete Sullivan, and others testifying before the Board of Inquiry, the days of remembering facts and stark terror of combat would begin in Danang at III MAF Headquarters and later in Pearl Harbor, Hawaii with the more formal inquiry by CINC Pacific Fleet. For HM1 Larry Lail and the crew of USS Acme involved in the handling of the remains and the search for the wreck of PCF-19, the memories and nightmares would begin and last for many years. Not knowing what happened to the men and who they were would haunt Larry Lail until 1995. For the divers involved in the search and recovery of the remains, the wondering about what sunk the boat and how the official findings of Sparrow Missiles could cause the damage witnessed by them underwater exploring the sunken boat for clues and remains. They too would have memories, both good and bad. For the pilots of the 480th Tactical Fighter Squadron, part of the 366 Tactical Fighter Wing known as "The Gunfighters", the memories of heavy aerial combat over the DMZ resulting in several "kills" being changed to "Friendly Fire" and blamed for the loss of Allied lives would be traumatic and affect them for many years. For the countless others, friends of these men and those who have not contacted me but carry a piece of this story in their memories to this day. For the family of Tony Chandler who carried the burden of "not knowing" for over twenty years as he was carried MIA and believed to have been killed by our forces in a "mistake", the feelings of helplessness are very hard to bear. For the family of Frank Bowman, this nightmare continues as he remains MIA and the waiting for some word that remains of their loved one could one day come home as did Tony Chandler. For this author, the story that has whirled around in my head for all these years and the yearning to tell this story may now be fulfilled.

CHAPTER FOURTEEN

Doc Lail Remembers

O ne of the key persons in this story and my best friend, the man who carried the heaviest burden can now provide his side of the story. HM1 Larry "Doc" Lail contacted Joe "Doc" Quartuccio by mail back in 1995 when he read in VFW magazine that he would be holding a "Swift Boat" reunion in Phoenix, Arizona. Larry could not attend but hoped someone there could shed some light on the unfinished tale in his head. This was the first time Larry had came across the term "Swift Boats" in many years and he did not know how large this reunion would be. However, he had a gut feeling that this time contact could be made with his past. As I overheard the conversation at breakfast between Doc Quartuccio and Jim Thomas, another Swiftie attending the reunion, the words "PCF-19 and June 1968" hit me like a two by four. It all came back to me in a rush. Thoughts, long forgotten, rushed through my head as this "very vivid" memory of that night became real again. Doc was asking Jim if he did not know about this incident would he put the word out at the Washington D.C. gathering of Swifties, which would be taking place in the next month. I interrupted them by asking if I could help.

"What do you know about this?" asked Doc Quartuccio?

"I was there, aboard PCF-12," I replied.

I took the information and called Doc Lail as soon as I returned from Phoenix to my home in San Diego, California. We talked for about four hours and I learned the following information.

He told me he was aboard USS Acme MSO-508 commanded by LCDR Merlin K. Overholser. He remembers being sent to the DMZ on June 16th, 1968 where divers boarded their ship to search for survivors and bodies of the crew of PCF-19. They had been hit by enemy fire and sunk near the border with North and South Vietnam. He remembers four men, three Caucasian and one oriental being recovered. USS Sanctuary sent LCM the first day and he sent the first body on it. One of the bodies was about 5ft 7in and had a black head of hair. Another body had a tattoo of a deer's head on his right upper arm. One body was fully clothed and had two sets of Vietnamese papers in his pocket. One man had a .38 cal pistol with a 6" blue steel barrel that was brought up by the divers. He filled out NAVMED N Death Certificates on each man listing all identifying marks. He transferred three bodies including the Vietnamese to an IUWG launch in Danang. He would like to find the names of these men, locate their families so he could tell them how sorry he was for their loss. He also wanted them to know that he handled their remains with the best care and utmost respect that he could under the conditions.

This was all he knew and had nightmares in which their faces would swim before his eyes as if to beckon him to find their names. Larry had spent two tours in Vietnam as a hospital corpsman with the Marines and had seen serious injury and death up close. Death was no stranger to him and he had dealt with most of those ghosts from his past in his own way. This was different and haunted him constantly. Seeing Doc Quartuccio's note in the VFW magazine offered a glimmer of hope and here we were, two voices out of the past discussing an incident that affected both of us very deeply. I would not meet Larry Lail face to face for a few years but we shared an instant bond that grew into a lasting friendship. I shared with him what I could over the phone about Swift Boats, their operations, the layout of the boat, and why things were where they were. It gave him a better picture in his mind of the conditions these men were in when they died. It wasn't until 1996 when I flew to the East Coast and met him in Norfolk for the first time. By this time we had located the skipper of PCF-19 and we all met in person for the first time. PCF-2, a restored training boat had been given to the Tidewater Community College for use as a geological survey vessel and except for removing the guns and painting it green was just like PCF-19 was when it was sunk. Walking through this boat and seeing it up close gave Doc Lail a new insight into what he had experienced and much of the terror in his mind began to ease itself. As the years went on, more and more witnesses would come forward. I would make a trip back to Vietnam in 1998 with LTJG John Davis, the skipper of PCF-19, Alex Radesa, a friend of Frank Bowman, and Major Richard Lennon, the Marine from 1st Amtracs. We shared our experiences with Larry and the story of that fateful night and the following several days aboard the Acme became much clearer.

Here then are the memories of Larry "Doc" Lail of the events surrounding the sinking of PCF-19. In his first letter to Jim Thomas, President of the new Swift Boat Sailors Association, dated June 4th, 1995, he would reveal much about himself and what transpired to this point. Here are excerpts from this letter.

A lamentable part of history is that those that made it are not around usually to discuss how it occurred. Joshua at Jericho, Jackson at Fredericksburg, the men listed on the Wall, the thousands of Americans whose remains are scattered throughout the world, would tell us (if alive) that we don't know the whole truth.

Twenty-seven years ago this month, I was riding the USS Acme (MSO-508) on Market Time Operations off the coast of Vietnam. It was my second tour in Southeast Asia. I had been there in 1965-66 ashore as a plank owner at NSA Danang. I arrived in country on October 14th, 1965. On October 27th, 1965 what was to be our hospital at NSA was destroyed when MAG-16 at China Beach was attacked. I was sent TAD to the 1st Marine Division until January of 1966 and returned to the USA at that time. I worked all facets of Trauma from ICU to Triage.

Figure 48. Larry "Doc" Lail in Danang Hospital, 1966.

It was a time of major injury yet great reward, and March of 1966 was a very bad period. There was a lot of heavy trauma from mines and booby traps. Men with no more than a head, chest, guts and maybe one arm survived. Amputations and coronary trauma were daily occurrences with multiple wounds being routine. Death was cheated and death prevailed. I learned how to deal with it and did my job.

In June of 1968 when we went North on the Acme for what I now know was the search for the 19 Swift Boat. I was the only man on board who had been to Vietnam before. Before leaving Long Beach in April of 1968, I had purchased two extra body bags, my IOL required two but I had four in my storeroom when we sailed. Thinking now in retrospect, without the two extras, I would not have had enough for the four men recovered from boat 19.

Once the boat was found, and the divers were working on the recovery, I just watched and waited. The boat was in a lagoon, not far out, maybe at most a mile or so off the beach. I wondered what had happened and my thoughts were that the 19 boat, like us had probably been interdicting boat traffic when it was sunk by the enemy. The divers however reported it was clear to them that the boat had probably been rocketed by aircraft. My thoughts then were that if the divers were right, boat 19 had probably detected significant movement, had called in an air strike, and had become a casualty of darkness and friendly fire. I remember thinking we've probably killed these guys through friendly fire and their bodies were intensively traumatized.

An article was in "Stars and Stripes" and came in our first mail call after we had concluded our search and recovery efforts and returned to our regular patrol area. Again, I changed my thinking as it explained or projected a possible explanation of what had happened to the boat and the men on it.

For almost 27 years, I have wondered about the true identities of the men I prepared death certificates on. In the past two days I have been able to obtain some answers and future hope. For this I have to thank Joe Quartuccio, Jim Steffes, and yourself. It now appears that one of the bodies I prepared the death certificate on was an Edward Cruz, EN2, USN; Hostile killed, North Vietnam, 16 June 1968. Jim Steffes got the info from a computer software history of the names appearing on the Vietnam Wall.

The divers off my boat said boat 19 was resting on the bottom in the same manner, as she would be on the surface. This means right side up on the bottom. Being real dark that night according to Jim, I wonder if the mouth of the lagoon was mistaken for the mouth of the river. The log of my ship, Acme, should report the exact location of where boat 19 was found and what we recovered from it. I examined the bodies and did the death certificates on the four bodies we recovered. Two men are known to have survived. How many were on the boat that night?

Until I talked with Joe Quartuccio and Jim Steffes, they did not know that the boat had been found or the bodies recovered. History—explanation has yet to be documented how many there were on boat 19 the night it was sunk. The survivors if found can also provide the names of those who were on board and close this chapter. I would be above all grateful for this info. At NSA, and with the Marines, all that I bagged and tagged went home and their families were able to know that they were truly dead. Those brought up off boat 19 offered little on scene identification prospects, ID cards, papers, logs, stencils and once having prepared their death certificates there is no Navy Policy whereby I would later be informed of their conclusions or disposition regarding the remains I had attended. I have therefore been left for almost 27 years wondering, "was identification finally and positively made and the next of kin notified?"

I guess in my own way, Jim, I carry these men as ghosts in my mind and I don't see my job as having been truly completed until their identities are known. I watch TV, listen to the radio, read something in the paper, Vietnam Senate hearings on POW/MIA's, chats with other Vietnam Vets, and they come back to mind. "History is incomplete".

It's like when you and I talked the other morning. You never leave your dead. NEVER! Despite what happens you go back for them. For me to be at peace, I had to know.

1) Who was the crew of boat 19, Name, rank, service number?
2) How many men were on board the night it was sunk?
3) Do those that survived, know that four dead were recovered?
4) What was the name of the dead man who had the tattoo of a buck deer's head on the upper arm?
5) Does anyone have the "need to know" of the exact location of boat 19 (See ship's log, USS Acme)
6) Why were such a heavily armored task force sent North to support the Acme during search and recovery of boat 19? Was it believed that we could also encounter air attack during this mission?

Jim Steffes had been in country only ten days when boat 19 went down. He was running his fourth patrol. Jim says the boat 19 people were a solid crew and to the best of his memory they had been together since training and in country since January 6th, 1968, a total of about nine months together. Jim the new guy, and the survivors of boat 19 seasoned men, both reported the same thing—Aircraft—probably Helos.

Looks to me like somebody in Danang or on up the ladder screwed up the night of the 16th and to later tell these men that it was lights of friendly ships on the horizon that they were shooting at is unbelievable after the deaths that occurred. Sin-Loi—which means "Sorry about that" just isn't enough. The crew, the survivors, the shipmates, the families, my ship and myself deserve better than that.

Key Reference Points recorded:

> Logs of USS Acme MSO-508 (I suggest June 16 to 21st, 1968)
> Logs of Coast Guard Vessel-Point Dume (June 15-16, 1968)
> USS Sanctuary—Hospital Ship (June 16-21, 1968)
> USS Constellation (CVA-64)
> USS Boston—Cruiser)
> Coast Guard Vessel Campbell
> BUMED, Washington, D.C. (For Death Certificates June 16-21, 1968 under
>   my name and Vietnam KIA's. NAV-MED-N's.

The Acme log is the key to the logs of other ships, as I cannot remember when we left our patrol area to go North or the exact day of our arrival. We were there on two consecutive days and the body composition of the remains we recovered would be consistent with men underwater from up to 96 hours after death. I am writing the names of the officers on board Acme in the event they appear in its log.

> Commanding Officer—Merlin K. Overholser, LCDR, USN
> Executive Officer—Richard C. Shell, LT, USNR
> Engineering Officer—Walter Turner, Ltjg, USN
> Ops Officer—   "?"   Abele, Ensign, USN
> Deck Officer—   "?"   Todd, Ensign, USN

The USS Acme was decommissioned in the mid 70's and salvaged out. There should be no great difficulty in gaining access to the Acme logs once it's relevance is explained. If there was a 7th man on board it could reveal also the best location for any MIA site. Explanations if such would be indicated. (Authors Note: These were the thoughts and recollections just after we made contact. Notice the reference to "boat 19" versus PCF-19 in later text. Of the list of questions Doc asked in this letter most have been answered by now. We know the names of the crew of boat 19; we know how many men were on board; those that survived know that four dead were recovered, not for certain. John D____ did not know until we told him and Anderegg died in a car crash in 1983, we never got to talk to him; we know the name of the dead man with the tattoo of a deer's head on his arm, we know the exact location of the boat 19 wreck, it is in the logs of Acme; what such a heavily armed task force sent to support Acme during the recovery? It was one and one half miles off the beach and five miles south of the Ben Hai River, which is the border between North and South Vietnam. At this time it was still not known what hit PCF-19 and there was still some heavy battles being waged ashore between the Marines and the NVA. Also, our naval ships were being shelled by batteries from just north of this position as well as Cua Viet being in the range of these guns. After Acme left the scene on June 17th, there was a round the clock bombing and shelling campaign to dislodge the gun positions and hopefully to destroy any aircraft on the ground. Sightings continued to occur for several weeks afterward into the month of August.)

On June 17th, about 2300, Acme transferred three bodies, identities unknown, to an IUWG Launch for transfer to the morgue at the Naval Hospital in Danang. When Larry Lail ordered copies of the mortuary logs in 1997 he was very surprised to find entries for GMG2 Billy Armstrong and EN2 Edward Cruz. In his notes to me, on February 25th, 1997, he describes the process this way.

In just the few days covered, the death that lived in Vietnam is evidenced. Unless I miscounted, one hundred and fifty two men went to the mortuary at Danang and ninety five of these were brought here by "C" Med, a field hospital near Danang similar to the MASH unit that got big TV coverage years ago. Two thirds of these dead were marines.

None of these pages provide any insight regards Anthony Gordon Chandler or Bui Quang Thi. (Authors Note: Although Larry says he delivered four bodies with paperwork, only two showed up on the logs. The Vietnamese is understandable because he did not

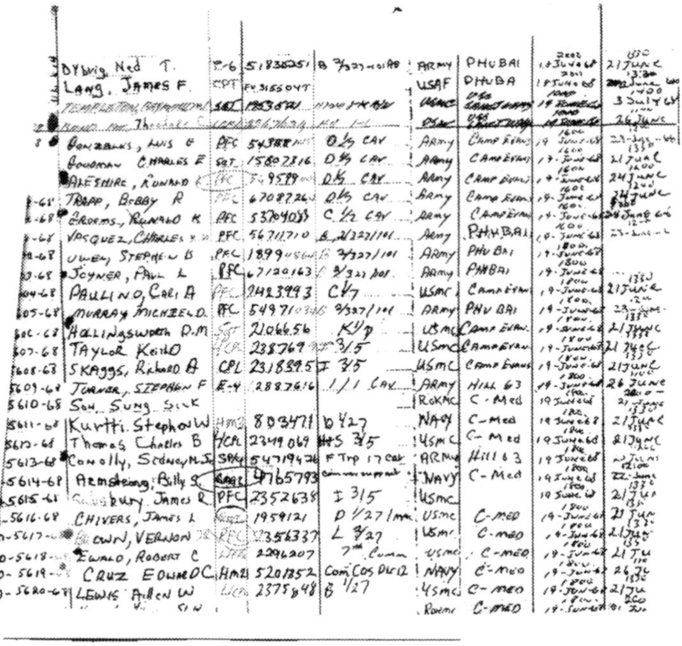

	DYbvig, Ned T.	E-6	51836251	B 3/327-101 AB	ARMY	PHU BAI	18 June 68	21 June
	Lang, James F.	CPT	FV3155047		USAF	PHU BA	18 June 68	[illegible] June
	[illegible]	SGT	[illegible]	[illegible]	USMC	[illegible]	19 [illegible]	3 July 68
	[illegible]				[illegible]	[illegible]	[illegible]	26 June
8	Gonzales, Luis G	PFC	54388[illegible]	D 1/5 CAV	Army	Camp Evans	19 June 68	23 June
	Bowman, Charles E	SGT	15807816	D 1/5 CAV	Army	Camp Evans	19 June 68	21 June
	Aleshire, Ronald E	PFC	[illegible]9599	D 1/5 CAV	Army	Camp Evans	19 June 68	24 June
-68	Trapp, Bobby R	PFC	67087726	D 1/5 CAV	Army	Camp Evans	19 June 68	24 June
-68	Grooms, Ronald K	PFC	53704033	C 1/2 CAV	Army	Camp Evans	19 June 68	28 June 68
-68	Vasquez, Charles	PFC	56711710	B 2/327/101	Army	PHU BAI	19 June 68	23 June
-68	Owen, Stephen B	PFC	1899[illegible]	B 3/327/101	Army	PHU BAI	19 June 68	
-68	Joyner, Paul L	PFC	67120163	3/327 101	Army	PHU BAI	19 June 68	
5604-68	Paulino, Carl A	PFC	2423993	C 1/7	USMC	Camp Evans	19 June 68	21 June
5605-68	Murray, Michael D.	PFC	54971[illegible]	3/327/101	Army	PHU BAI	19 June 68	23 June
5606-68	Hollingsworth D.M	Sgt	2106656	K 1/9	USMC	Camp Evans	19 June 68	21 June
5607-68	Taylor Keith O	LCPL	238769	3/5	USMC	Camp Evans	19 June 68	21 June
5608-68	Skaggs, Richard A	CPL	2318395	I 3/5	USMC	Camp Evans	19 June 68	21 June
5609-68	Turner, Stephen F	E-4	2887616	1/1 CAV	Army	Hill 63	19 June 68	26 June
5610-68	Son, Sung Sik				ROKMC	C-Med	19 June 68	21 June
5611-68	Kurtti, Stephen W	HM3	803471	D 1/27	NAVY	C-Med	19 June 68	21 June
5612-68	Thomas, Charles B	LCPL	2349069	H&S 3/5	USMC	C-Med	19 June 68	21 June
5613-68	Conolly, Sidney M. Jr	SP4	54719476	F Trp 17 Cav	ARMY	Hill 63	19 June 68	21 June
5614-68	Armstrong, Billy S.	GMG2	4765793	[illegible]	NAVY	C-Med	19 June 68	22 June
5615-68	[illegible]bury, James R	PFC	2352638	I 3/5	USMC		19 June 68	21 June
5616-68	Chivers, James L	[illegible]	1959121	D 1/27 1st Mar	USMC	C-Med	19 June 68	21 June
5617-68	Brown, Vernon	PFC	2356337	L 3/27	USMC	C-Med	19 June 68	21 June
5618-68	Ewald, Robert C	[illegible]	2296207	7th Comm	USMC	C-Med	19 June 68	21 June
5619-68	Cruz Edward C	HM2	5201352	Com Cos Div 12	NAVY	C-Med	19 June 68	26 June
5620-68	Lewis Allen W	LCPL	2375848	B 1/27	USMC	C-Med	19 June 68	21 June
	[illegible]				ROKMC	C-Med	19 June	[illegible]

Figure 49. Danang Mortuary Logs Page six, June 19th, 1968.

have to go through this facility but is assumed to have been turned over to the Vietnamese Navy Command for return to his family. Billy Armstrong was sent to Sanctuary on June 16th and Edward Cruz was turned over on June 17th along with Anthony Chandler.) Although we do have records of Billy Armstrong being transferred to the USS Sanctuary, these logs record his body as being received by "C" Med at 1800 on June 19th, about 96 hours after

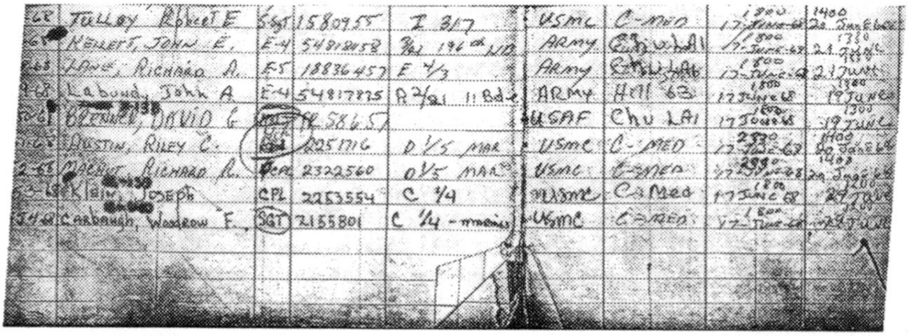

Figure 50. Danang Mortuary Logs, Page Three, June 17th, 1968.

his recovery by divers. Of the other bodies recovered, taken to Danang, and turned over to a motor launch that came out to meet Acme at 2300 on June 17th, the only one recorded is Edward Cruz. Cruz is also recorded as being received at Danang Mortuary at 1800 on June 19th. Cruz's service number and command are correct but his rate is not. He is listed as HM2 when he was an EN2.

A review of these log notations will reveal that "C" Med routinely and daily transported the dead to the Danang Mortuary. There is with the exception of two notations, a routine time in which they did this. The logs will reveal (exception Page 3) that this occurred regularly at 1600 or 1800 hours. On page three, you will note two entries inserted which break the 1800-hour sequence. These two notations are recorded as the bodies of two Marines.

Austin, Riley C. Ser# 2251716, USMC
Machut, Richard R. Ser# 2322560, USMC.

Once these two bodies are reported, the log goes back to recording nine more bodies at 1800 hours on the 17th, and then continues on the 18th and many are recorded on that day. On June 19th, and on page six shown on a previous page, two of PCF-19 crew are recorded as being received at Danang Mortuary at 1800 hours on June 19th. One of these was recovered on June 16th and transferred to Sanctuary and one of the others recovered on June 17th and brought into Danang at 2300 hours on June 17th.

As I looked at the 2330 entries on Page 3, I wondered why two marines from "D" Company, 1st Battalion, 5th Marines were not only out of context in time, but also wondered why "C" Med would deliver them that late on the 17th as they would be coming again on the 18th.

Having transferred the Acme bodies at 2300 on the 17th, knowing that the Danang Mortuary was less than seven miles away, at the most 15 minutes travel time. I still cannot figure out how either Cruz or Armstrong did not get to the Mortuary by the 17 of June and am completely baffled as to how both of these bodies ended up in "C" Med and then being transferred to Danang Mortuary on June 19th at 1800 hours. The PCF-19 crew lost their lives at approximately 0100 hours on the 16th of June. The receipted time in the log of two of the crew, Armstrong and Cruz is 89 hours after the sinking. Where were these men after 2300 hours on June 17th? I cannot explain it! Just accounting for Cruz and putting Chandler, Armstrong and Bui Quang Thi aside, it took Cruz 44 hours from his Acme transfer to the morgue notation at 1800 hours on the 19th. When he was transferred from the Acme, he was no more than 30 minutes, a short drive, and in a direct line. Why wasn't he or the others transferred there? I don't know, and speculation won't solve anything.

It should be noted that the references listed previously in the Boston logs and the Hobart being hit on the 17th. In the above listed mortuary log you will note that the two

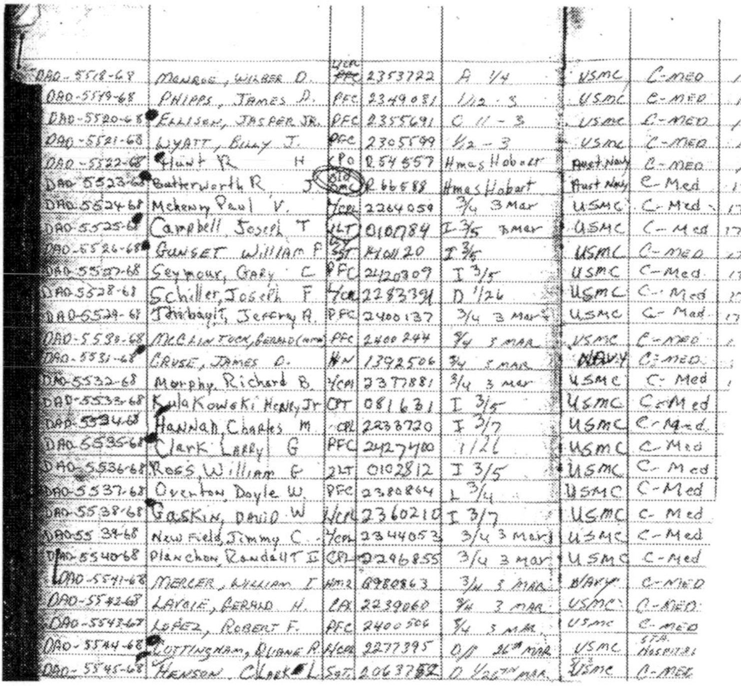

Figure 51. Danang Mortuary Logs Page Two, June 17th, 1968.

Australian Sailors killed on Hobart are listed on Page two above on lines 5 and 6. These men were killed in the early hours of the 17th, were in the Danang Mortuary, having been brought there by "C" Med on the same day they lost their lives, June 17th.

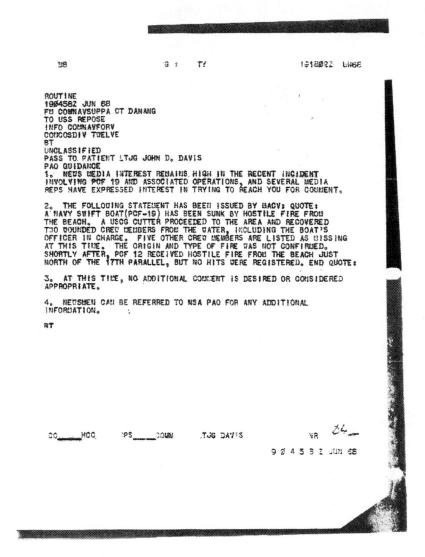

```
UB                 G Y   TY              191802Z LN68

ROUTINE
190458Z JUN 68
FM COMNAVSUPPA CT DANANG
TO USS REPOSE
INFO COMNAVFORV
COMCOSDIV TUELVE
BT
UNCLASSIFIED
PASS TO PATIENT LTJG JOHN D. DAVIS
PAO GUIDANCE
1.  NEWS MEDIA INTEREST REMAINS HIGH IN THE RECENT INCIDENT
INVOLVING PCF 19 AND ASSOCIATED OPERATIONS, AND SEVERAL MEDIA
REPS HAVE EXPRESSED INTEREST IN TRYING TO REACH YOU FOR COMMENT.

2.  THE FOLLOWING STATEMENT HAS BEEN ISSUED BY MACV: QUOTE:
A NAVY SWIFT BOAT(PCF-19) HAS BEEN SUNK BY HOSTILE FIRE FROM
THE BEACH.  A USCG CUTTER PROCEEDED TO THE AREA AND RECOVERED
TWO WOUNDED CREW MEMBERS FROM THE WATER, INCLUDING THE BOAT'S
OFFICER IN CHARGE.  FIVE OTHER CREW MEMBERS ARE LISTED AS MISSING
AT THIS TIME.  THE ORIGIN AND TYPE OF FIRE WAS NOT CONFIRMED.
SHORTLY AFTER, PCF 12 RECEIVED HOSTILE FIRE FROM THE BEACH JUST
NORTH OF THE 17TH PARALLEL, BUT NO HITS WERE REGISTERED.  END QUOTE:

3.  AT THIS TIME, NO ADDITIONAL COMMENT IS DESIRED OR CONSIDERED
APPROPRIATE.

4.  NEWSMEN CAN BE REFERRED TO NSA PAO FOR ANY ADDITIONAL
INFORMATION.

BT

CO____HCO   PS____COMM   .TJG DAVIS        VR  64
                                       9 0 4 5 3 2 JUN 68
```

Figure 52. Message of June 19th, 1968 to LTJG John Davis.

(Authors Note: A message received by Ltjg John Davis on USS Repose and dated the 19th of June stated that Public Affairs was still listing the crew as missing. This message was delivered in the early hours of June 19th, 1968. All bodies recovered were on their way to mortuary services no later than 2300 on June 17th.

The Public Affairs Office was certainly aware of the recovery, as message traffic verifies it. Yet they kept a stated release that was policy for some unknown reason. The message also advised John Davis not to comment to the media on the events and to refer them to Naval Support Activity Public Affairs Officer for any additional information. In other words "don't talk to anyone about this".)

(Larry Lail continues) I had hoped that the logs would provide some conclusive answers but they haven't. They pose as many questions as existed before. Chandler and Bui Quang Thi are not recorded, yet somehow Cruz got there on the 19th after being transferred by the Acme at 2300 on the 17th.

These and other questions will continue to elude the investigators until a more formative answer can be found. Until this occurs by POW/MIA Offices, we will be left to wonder.

(Authors Note: As the above activities played out at the Danang Mortuary, it seemed that all the men were accounted for on PCF-19. Official message traffic following the incident and one of the divers, DP1 Arnold Fellers, reported a total of three bodies recovered, one on June 16th and two more on June 17th. They were as yet unidentified by June 17th, however they were described as one Vietnamese, one Caucasian, and one Malaysian. HM1 Larry Lail and one of the motor whaleboat crew state that one was recovered on June 16th and delivered to USS Sanctuary at sea. This body was Caucasian. On the 17th, three more were recovered and laid side by side on the stern of Acme in body bags. Larry Lail would also state that he carried four body bags on board and used them all. The last three would include a Caucasian, an Oriental/American, and a fully clothed Vietnamese with two sets of Vietnamese papers on him. These three bodies would be delivered to Danang and placed aboard an IUWG motor launch for transfer. This took place approximately 2300 on June 17th.

Larry Lail says that it was his duty as an independent duty corpsman, in the absence of a Medical Officer on board, to properly document these remains based on the information he had. He believes that new death certificates were prepared in Danang once the identities of the remains were known and his papers would be destroyed. This is a normal practice and does not bother him. What bothers him is that four bodies were delivered from his vessel and only three arrive at their destination.

CHAPTER FIFTEEN

The Aftermath of the Search and Recovery

In the days following the completion of the Search and Recovery Operation, the men at all levels of command tried to sort out the details of what happened in these three days and nights.

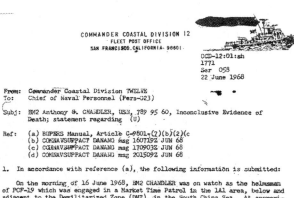

COMMANDER COASTAL DIVISION 12
FLEET POST OFFICE
SAN FRANCISCO, CALIFORNIA. 96601

CCD-12:01:sh
1771
Ser 058
22 June 1968

From: Commander Coastal Division TWELVE
To: Chief of Naval Personnel (Pers-G23)

Subj: BM2 Anthony G. CHANDLER, USN, 789 95 60, Inconclusive Evidence of Death; statement regarding (U)

Ref: (a) BUPERS Manual, Article C-9801-(7)(b)(2)(c
(b) COMNAVSUPPACT DANANG msg 160719Z JUN 68
(c) COMNAVSUPPACT DANANG msg 170903Z JUN 68
(d) COMNAVSUPPACT DANANG msg 201509Z JUN 68

1. In accordance with reference (a), the following information is submitted:

On the morning of 16 June 1968, BM2 CHANDLER was on watch as the helmsman of PCF-19 which was engaged in a Market Time Patrol in the 1A1 area, below and adjacent to the Demilitarized Zone (DMZ), in the South China Sea. At approximately 0030H on the morning of the 16th, PCF-19 was attacked by unknown airborne units. PCF-19 suffered two direct hits with rockets of unknown size. One rocket went directly through the pilothouse close by BM2 CHANDLER and exploded in the forward cabin directly below BM2 CHANDLER. Eye witness reports by the Officer-in-Charge of PCF-19, who was on watch at the time of the attack, states that when the rocket in the pilot house hit, the OINC saw BM2 CHANDLER stand straight up as the rocket hit. No further knowledge of BM2 CHANDLER's actions or disposition could be given by either the OINC, who was temporarily blinded, or the other survivor, who was on watch as the lookout and forward gunner at the time of the attack. PCF-19 sank at Lat 16° 59'N Long 117° 38'E in 42 feet of water, within 4 minutes after the attack. PCF-12 and the USCGC PT DUME combined in rescue operations, although both were coming under heavy attack by enemy aircraft. USCGC PT DUME rescued the two known survivors who were MEDEVACED to the USS REPOSE (AH-16). Continued searches by PCF-12, USCGC PT DUME, SAR Aircraft, and shore elements of the 3rd Marine Division on 16 June failed to discover any further survivors. On 17, 18, 19 and 20 June, PCF-80 in 1A1 failed to discover any additional survivors or bodies in the water. Divers from the EOD detachment NSAD, Cua Viet dove on PCF-19 on 17, 18, 19 and 20 June and recovered 3 bodies from the craft. Eye witness statements as to the fate of one additional crewmember confirms that individual's death. On 20 June PCF-19 was destroyed by the EOD detachment and the official search for survivors was terminated.

2. In view of the information obtained by personal interviews of the survivors of PCF-19, the condition of the remains of the crewmembers recovered from PCF-19 and pictures taken of the hull of PCF-19 showing the results of the explosions, it is the opinion of this command that BM2 CHANDLER was killed instantaneously by the exploding rocket and thrown clear of PCF-19. In the possibility that BM2 CHANDLER was not instantaneously killed by the explosion, the condition of those

9

Figure 53. Letter from CosDiv Twelve to NAVPERS of June 22nd.

Now a letter from CosDiv12 to Chief Naval Personnel would reveal a major change and explain the loss of one body, that of Chandler.

1771
Ser 058

bodies recovered from PCF-19 would indicate that BM2 CHANDLER could not have survived any prolonged exposure to the elements successfully.

3. This command recommends that the status of BM2 Anthony C. CHANDLER, USN, 789 95 60 be changed from mission in action to killed in action as a direct result of hostile fire.

I..M. BAILEY

Copy to:
COMCOSRON ONE
COMNAVSUPPACT DANANG

Figure 54. Letter from CosDiv 12 to NAVPERS of June 22nd, page 2.

Based on the information obtained by personal interviews of the survivors, the condition of the remains of the crewmembers recovered from PCF-19, and pictures taken of the hull of PCF-19 showing the results of the explosions, it is of the opinion of this command that BM2 Chandler was killed instantaneously by the exploding rocket and thrown clear of PCF-19. In the possibility that the explosion did not kill BM2 Chandler instantly, the condition of those bodies recovered from PCF-19 would indicate that BM2 Chandler could not have survived any prolonged exposure to the elements successfully. This command recommends that the status of BM2 Anthony C. Chandler be changed from missing in action to killed in action as a direct result of hostile fire. This is signed by I.M. Bailey, Lt, USN, Commander Coastal Division Twelve.

The problem with this diagnosis is it is not based on anything other than "lack of evidence". The divers did not report any windows or hatches blown out in the pilothouse. Ltjg John Davis was standing less than three feet from him and was blinded by the blast but only knocked to his knees from which he immediately stood up and exited the boat via the port hatch. Since most of the damage was confined to the forward cabin under the pilothouse, it is unlikely that the explosion would have killed Chandler and blown him clear of the boat. His body, according to Doc Lail was missing a leg but not as seriously damaged as the ones in the forward cabin.

The fact that the divers recovered a pistol, which was a personal weapon of Chandler's and that it was intact means they entered the pilothouse. Although the one diver reported only three bodies recovered, that was by him and he found them inside the main cabin. He says they were lying in the bunks. There were two bunks in the main cabin. The publications and codebooks recovered would have been in the pilothouse as well. Larry Lail asked the diver cleaning the pistol what he was going to do with it since it obviously was a personal weapon and did not belong to the Navy as part of the boats weapons. His reply was, "I will keep it I guess, he doesn't need it anymore." This comment would lead me to believe he took it off a body that he recovered. If it was lying loose in the boat and it belonged to one of the two survivors, he could get in serious trouble for keeping it. I believe he felt safe keeping it since he did take it off a dead body, that of BM2 Chandler. I cannot prove this of course, I leave it to the reader to arrive at the same conclusion Larry Lail and I came to.

Mr. Jack Young, stepfather of Anthony Chandler refused to believe that his stepson had been killed next to the seriously injured boat skipper and be blown clear of the boat. He continued to press the government for more and better answers. He had been in the military and worked for the Defense Department and had a good idea how things worked and also that things in wartime could go very wrong. Sometime after September 1973, a letter from Commander, US Army Memorial Affairs Agency in Washington, D.C. would come to the Young Family. It summed up the information to date stating he was on routine patrol and artillery or rocket fire from the land caused the boat to explode. The craft sank near the DMZ and BM2 Chandler was not seen or heard from again. An extensive search was conducted and two survivors were picked up in the immediate area. Determination of death was received on 22 June 1968. (Authors Note: This conflicts with the earlier findings of "friendly fire" and say the boat was hit by shore fire and exploded. Not true or even close and only made the Young family more suspicious that something was not right with this case.)

It further states that an Overwater/At Sea Casualty Resolution Operation was conducted during the period of July through September 1973 to determine the feasibility/desirability of expanded At Sea Casualty Resolution Operation to be used in cases such as that described in the foregoing. Based on the lack of any positive results whatsoever, the At Sea Operations were terminated. (Authors Note: What this means is a sea search was made either by air or on the water to determine if a more extensive search of the area be made as part of an operation. At this time Summer of 1973, the North Vietnamese had moved south towards Quang Tri in the north, Kontum in the highlands, and An Loc just sixty miles north of Saigon. Negotiations in Paris failed to dislodge the NVA and the South Vietnamese Government could not defeat them without American forces. In January 1973 a "Peace with Honor" agreement was signed in Paris and it allowed the North Vietnamese to remain in South Vietnam.

JCRC-CDD-CR

SUBJECT: Change of Category from "Dead (BNR)" to "Remains Nonrecoverable"

Commander
US Army Memorial Affairs Agency
Tempo A Building
Washington, DC 20315

1. According to available information, Anthony Gordon CHANDLER, DATA   ,
BM2, USN, was a crew member aboard a PCF 19, operating in the South China Sea.
On 16 June 1968 the craft was on a routine patrol when artillery or rocket
fire from the land caused it to explode. The craft sank near the DMZ and
BM2 CHANDLER was not seen or heard from again. An extensive search was conducted and two survivors were picked up in the immediate area. Determination
of death was received on 22 June 1968.

2. An Overwater/At Sea Casualty Resolution Operation was conducted during the
period of July through September 1973 to determine the feasibility/desirabilit;
of expanded At Sea Casualty Resolution Operation to be used in cases such as
that described in the foregoing. Based on the lack of any positive results
whatsoever, the At Sea Operations were terminated. An additional factor considered was that the continuation of Operations under these conditions could
serve to generate false expectations of families concerned.

3. No record of burial is on file for the above casualty

4. Findings and recommendations are based on all available information.

5. It is recommended that the remains of the subject deceased be considered
nonrecoverable and that all records pertaining to search and recovery be place
in an inactive status.

                    JOSEPH R. ULATOSKI
                    Brigadier General, USA
                    Commanding

Figure 55. Letter Changing Chandler's status from KIA-BNR to KIA—
Remains not Recoverable.

An underwater search of PCF-19 would have created an incident and public outcry from Hanoi. POW's were still being held and Peace Talks were going on. Obviously there was no underwater search of PCF-19 or even attempts to dive on the wreck to look for more remains. This letter was to pacify the family but actually served to confuse the issue even further.) The letter goes on to state, "An additional factor considered was that the continuation of operations under these conditions could serve to generate false expectations of families concerned." It is recommended that the remains of the subject deceased be considered non recoverable and that all records pertaining to search and recovery be placed in an inactive status. Signed Joseph R. Ulatoski, Brigadier General, USA Commanding.

(Authors Note: This was supposed to end it all and put it to rest forever. I believe many of these letters were sent to families to attempt to shorten the list of MIA's by changing their status to "remains not recoverable". It was a time in our history when America just wanted to forget Vietnam and all the pain that went with it. Well, the Young family still felt the pain and felt cheated by the government that took their son. The Bowman family did not receive one of these letters, however, just the one back in 1968 that listed their son as MIA. Years went by and they did not receive any updates. The Young family received some information, mostly "we will get back to you" because Jack Young kept writing letters and asking questions. The Bowman family continued to grieve in silence, and to this day have only received that one letter listing him as MIA. There were no "changes in status" for Frank Bowman; he continued to be listed as MIA. John Anderegg stated that Bowman got clear of the boat, died in his arms on the raft and floated away losing an arm when the current took him from Anderegg. He could not hold on to John Davis and Bowman at the same time. So this means there was no need to look any further for remains of Frank Bowman? Let's just carry him "Missing in Action".

Why didn't a search of the wreck of PCF-19 take place after the war ended in 1975 and the POW's came home? QM2 Frank Bowman was not among the POW's released nor was he listed in any North Vietnamese Records as being captured or even found. If his body washed up on shore inside North Vietnam in June 1968, the local people could have buried him without ceremony. Since he was dead, he was of no value to the government and more than likely was not reported above the village chief level.)

Well, the story doesn't end here for sure. On September 15th, 1993, a letter from the Navy to the Young Family included a copy of a "Case Narrative" passed to the Vietnamese Government during a meeting on July 28th, 1993. It contained the case data on the PCF-19 sinking and gave personal details on two missing servicemen, BM2 Anthony Chandler and QM2 Frank Bowman. This was to assist them in investigating the missing men.

On November 30th, 1993, a copy of the Joint Task Force (JTF-FA) Field Investigation Report was sent to the Young Family. It contained the details of an investigation into the incident of June 16th, 1968, which resulted in the two men being Missing in Action. It states that their patrol boat was sunk by probable artillery fire approximately three kilometers off shore. The team interviewed a total of five witnesses. Two with first hand information regarding the sinking of a U.S. Patrol Boat in 1968 and three others who claim to have scavenged the wreckage of a U.S. Patrol Boat three Kilometers offshore. One of these witnesses gave the team a military identification card and a bone fragment, both of which were reportedly retrieved from the wreckage. The identification card does not correlate to any unaccounted for individuals. The remains fragment was turned over the VNOSMP to be forwarded to Hanoi for Joint Forensic review. The team traveled by boat to the area witnesses indicated the shipwreck was located and recorded the grid coordinates. The team also traveled to the grid coordinates held in U.S. Records for the incident. (The two sites are within one kilometer of each other). The team was unable to determine whether or not there was evidence of a shipwreck at either site. Divers from Thang Loi Hamlet, Ky Anh District, Ha Tinh Province reportedly recovered a dog tag from the wreckage. Request Vietnamese Officials attempt to locate these individuals for interviews. Recommend this case for reinvestigation.

On 23 August 1993, the Joint Team investigated case 1210 in Trung Giang (Trung Giang) Village, Gio Linh District, Quang Tri Province. The team interviewed three witnesses with

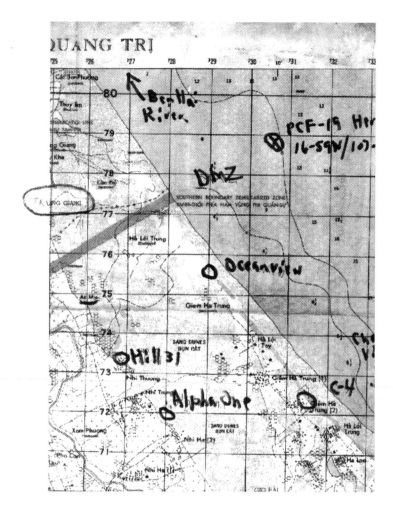

Figure 56. Chart of DMZ Area Showing Location of Trung Giang Village.

information possibly correlating to this case. The first witness, Mr. Hoang Ngoc Dung is a 48 year old adult, is currently the Trung Giang Village Chairman and was a member of the Village Militia during the war. He related the following:

1) At approximately 0100 hours on an unknown date in the summer of 1968, Mr. Dung was manning his combat position when he witnessed a U.S. Patrol Boat approximately three kilometers offshore get struck by coastal artillery fire. The vessel sank immediately.

(Authors note: This village is inside the southern half of the DMZ and should not have had any villagers or militia in it. The NVA moved around this area at will and fought with U.S. Marines nightly. The man could not have been a part of the village militia.) There was no fire or explosion. Following the sinking, Mr. Dung did not see any rescue aircraft arrive in the area and to his knowledge, no bodies ever washed ashore at any time following the incident. (Authors note: This contradicts all the testimony of the American witnesses who said the Naval presence was formidable with day and night bombing of the area. However, it is not the first time the North Vietnamese Government exaggerated the accounts of battle or the amount of U.S. Casualties to men and material.)

2) Mr. Dung heard that in March 1991, Mr. Bui Xuan Tao had salvaged scrap metal from the wreckage of the sunken patrol boat. During the salvaging, divers claimed there were human remains still in the wreckage. Mr. Dung also heard that a Mr. Phan Thu recovered a plastic identification card, which he still has.

The Team next interviewed Mr. Bui Xuan Tao, a 30-year-old adult fisherman who provided the following testimony:

1) In April 1991, Mr. Tao hired two divers from Ha Tinh Province to salvage scrap metal from the wreck of a boat, which was sunk at a depth of approximately 15 meters. Mr. Tao had known the location of the wreck since 1972-73 and he had heard that it was a U.S. Patrol Boat that was sunk by artillery fire in 1967-68.

2) Mr. Tao used his fishing boat to take the divers to the wreck location, but Mr. Tao himself remained on the boat while the divers went down to salvage the wreckage. The two divers, Mr. Ngu and Mr. Nhoe, (the witness did not know the individuals' full names), recovered a propeller and some aluminum from the wreckage. During the salvage operation, the divers told Mr. Tao that there were many small human remains (approximately finger-size) in the wreck near the boat's helm. The divers did not recover any of the remains, but Mr. Ngu recovered a dog tag, which Mr. Tao let him keep. Mr. Tao does not know what name or other data was on the dog tag.

3) Mr. Ngu and Mr. Nhoe currently reside in Thang Loi Hamlet, Ky Anh District, Ha Tinh Province. Mr. Tao could not recall the name of the village, but said it was located along the coast. (Authors note: Here you see evidence that there are still remains on board the PCF-19 and based on the description of the bodies recovered could be any or all of the men recovered including some from QM2 Frank Bowman.

The third witness interviewed was Mr. Pham Tram, a 55-year-old adult fisherman and resident of Nam Son Hamlet, Trung Giang Village. From 1966 to 1972, Mr. Tram was a member of the village militia. He related the following:

1) At approximately 1500 hours on an unknown date in June 1968, Mr. Tram saw a small U.S. Warship get struck by coastal artillery fire about five kilometers offshore.

The ship caught fire and headed away from the coast. Using binoculars, Mr. Tram saw the ship sink when it was about 12-15 kilometers offshore.

2) Mr. Tram also saw several helicopters in the area of the ship when it sank, but saw no other ships. He does not know whether anyone was rescued from the ship, and he has no knowledge of any bodies ever washing ashore in the area following the incident.

(Authors note: This could not have been PCF-19 because it occurred in the daytime, but again notice the reference to coastal artillery fire, no mention of NVA helicopters and this man also was in the village militia of an abandoned village inside the DMZ. If they were friendly to the South they would have been evacuated. If friendly to the North, they would have been killed in one of the skirmishes with the Marines along the front lines.

Mr. Tram would also describe an incident in the summer of 1972 involving an F-4 fighter plane shot down and crashed into the ocean. One pilot was rescued by helicopters and the other captured by the militia and turned over to authorities. Since the attack by the NVA into South Vietnam began in January 1972, this area would have been repopulated and thus had a militia. The pilot captured was later released in 1975 with the POW's. So part of his testimony was factual but the first part involving the sinking of a small warship was pure fiction.)

On 31 August 1993, the team returned to the investigation of this case. The team interviewed two additional witnesses. The first witness was Mr. Phan Van Thu, a 57-year-old adult fisherman who had been mentioned by Mr. Dung during his interview. Mr. Thu related the following:

1) In July 1991, Mr. Thu and his son, Mr. Phan Van Thong, salvaged scrap metal from a shipwreck approximately three kilometers offshore. He indicated that the wreck was the same one that Mr. Tao had described. Mr. Thu had no knowledge of the circumstances in which the vessel was sunk.

2) Mr. Thu's son, Mr. Thong, had done the actual diving near the wreckage and had found a military identification card, which Mr. Thu subsequently turned over to IE2. Field analysis indicates the identification card is not associated with any unaccounted for personnel. (Authors note: This identification card turned out to belong to LTJG John Davis, the skipper of PCF-19.) Mr. Thu also claimed his son had recovered a portion of a leg bone from the wreckage which they took home and buried. He still has the bone at his home and agreed to turn it over to IE2. (Authors note: This bone fragment was confirmed by DNA analysis to belong to BM2 Anthony Chandler and was returned to his family. These remains were buried in Warner Robbins, GA, on June 16th, 2001, exactly 33 years after he was killed.)

3) Mr. Thu also stated that his son found many other remains fragments inside the wreckage, but did not retrieve them. (Authors note: Here is further evidence that

possible remains of QM2 Frank Bowman are on board the wreckage and can easily be retrieved.)

IE2 next interviewed Mr. Phan Van Thong, the 36-year-old adult son of Mr. Thu. Mr. Thong provided the same testimony as Mr. Thu and added that the wreckage was that of a small patrol boat. At the time they salvaged the wreckage, the highest point of the bow was approximately two meters below the surface of the water. (Authors note: This could have been caused by the explosions during the salvage of the scrap metal from the hull putting air inside the wreckage causing it to shift. It was originally described by the Navy divers in 1968 as resting on the bottom just like it would set on the surface of the water.) Mr. Thong said that much of the boat's aluminum and stainless steel structure has been salvaged and what presently remains is mostly covered with sand and silt. (Authors note: It sounds like time and the ocean are covering the evidence and unless we act quickly, all the remaining remains will be lost. Locating the wreck again and recovering the mud and debris from inside the boat so the remains can be retrieved should be a top priority.)

None of the witnesses interviewed regarding this case had any knowledge of bodies ever washing ashore in the area. They also claimed to have no knowledge of any capture incidents, remains, gravesites, or Americans remaining in Vietnam following the war. (Authors note: This should not be surprising since as I said earlier, this Trung Giang Village was abandoned during 1968 and was part of a constant battle zone until the Americans departed in 1971 leaving the South Vietnamese Army to defend the DMZ.)

Following the final two interviews, IE2, accompanied by Mr. Tao, Mr. Thu and Mr. Thong, traveled by boat to the area in which they indicated the wreck was located (48QYD30827877) IE2 then proceeded to the Grid Coordinates held in U.S. Records as the incident location (48QYD305795). The team was unable to determine whether any wreckage was located at either site. (Authors note: Since they were already there in a boat and the boat wreckage was in approximately 15 fathoms of water, that is 90 feet and the bow was only two meters below the surface of the water, why didn't anyone dive down to verify the wreck location and its condition. Instead the word of these Vietnamese fishermen and divers was taken and never checked out.)

After returning from the site surveys, IE2 traveled to Mr. Thu's home in Hamlet 9 (Grid Coordinates: 48QYD28367627), Trung Giang Village. Mr. Thu gave the team a bone fragment, which was allegedly recovered from the shipwreck. IE2 took custody of the fragment, photographed it, and subsequently turned it over to the VNOSMP to be forwarded to Hanoi for Joint Forensic Review.

During the course of this investigation, IE2 randomly questioned residents of Trung Giang Village and its coastal hamlets from the mouth of the Ben Hai River down to and including Hamlet 9 in an attempt to locate additional witnesses regarding this case. The team was unable to locate anyone with knowledge of the incident or knowledge of remains having ever washed ashore in the area. (Authors note: Again there is inconsistency in that this boat was supposedly sunk by coastal artillery and only two men witnessed it. No other witnesses could be found from the area that had any knowledge of this case. I repeat, since the village was abandoned in 1968 there could not have been any witnesses including Mr. Thu and Mr. Tram.)

Material evidence: The following items were obtained by IE2 during the investigation of case 1210:

1) One faded military identification card, information was researched by IE2, the information on the ID card does not correlate to any unaccounted for personnel. Data will be passed via separate correspondence. (Authors note: The ID card belonged to LTJG John Davis.)
2) One remains fragment (possibly femur), measuring 10.5 X 8.5 centimeters.

Survey results: On 31 August 1993, IE2 surveyed the area identified by the witnesses and the incident location reported by U.S. Sources—The Global Positioning System, tracking four satellites, was used for site verification. Related data is as follows:

1) Project Area: The witness-reported site is located at Grid Coordinates 48QYD30827877 and the location is at Grid Coordinates 48QYD305795. Map data is as follows: Map Name—Quang Tri, Map sheet—6442 IV, map series L7014, printed 1969.
2) Outstanding features: Sites are approximately three kilometers off the coast of Trung Giang Village, Gio Linh District, Quang Tri Province. The depth of the ocean in the project area is approximately 15 (as reported by the witnesses).
3) Terrain: N/A
4) Soil Condition: N/A
5) Vegetation: N/A
6) Method of Search: The team traveled by boat to the sites but was unable to see any wreckage in the area.
7) Hazards: No hazards present at this time.

Recommended future actions:

1) Recommend JTF-FA J2 attempt to determine whether the individual listed on the identification card provided by Mr. Thu, was a crewman aboard the vessel associated with case 1210.
2) Recommend VNOSMP attempt to locate Mr. Ngu and Mr. Nhoe of Thang Loi Hamlet, Ky Anh District, Ha Tinh Province in order to make them available for interview regarding this case and to determine whether they are in possession of a dog tag related to this case.

3) Pending results of the above recommendations and further analysis, recommend JTF-FA research the feasibility of an underwater survey of the alleged wreckage location.
4) Pertinent location or data changes: None.
5) Areas or case file information not investigated: None.
6) Analyst comments:

   A. All witnesses interviewed regarding this case seemed straightforward with their responses and did not appear to be attempting to mislead or deceive the team.
   B. Although there are discrepancies between two of the witnesses first hand accounts of the incident, the general circumstances and time frame seem to correlate to case 1210.
   C. The wreckage site indicated by the witnesses is less than one kilometer from the coordinates held in U.S. Records. A grid search of all losses in the area revealed no ships or boats sunk within a ten-kilometer radius of the incident location. Thus, there is a good probability that the wreckage the witnesses found was that of the vessel associated with this case.
   D. In view of the above information and the high probability of remains at the witness site, it is recommended that the divers in the Ha Tinh Province be interviewed regarding the case and also to attempt to obtain or view the dog tags allegedly in their possession, for correlation to this case.
   E. Investigation of this case in Quang Tri Province is complete. The recommendation for reinvestigation is directed at the divers in Ha Tinh Province. If the information correlates to this case and the witnesses are firm in their belief that remains are at the site, the next step would be a feasibility assessment for recovery of the site.
   F. Search and Recovery Specialist comments: Recommend further action at the incident location; await the results of a feasibility study on underwater recovery of the site.
   G. Team Chief Comments: Most of the information obtained during this investigation generally correlates with the circumstances of loss for case 1210. Surveys of the witness-reported site and the incident location in U.S. Records were inconclusive. Also recommend Vietnamese Officials attempt to locate Mr. Ngu and Mr. Nhoe (alleged to have seen human remains in the wreckage and recovered a dog tag from the same site) in Ky Anh District, Ha Tinh Province. If the information derived from those witnesses correlates to this case, a feasibility assessment for underwater recovery of this site would be the next step. Recommend this case for reinvestigation.

(Authors Note: The above transcript was taken word for word from the original document except for the names of the team members.

I also left out a testimony of a witness giving details of an unrelated case involving an aircraft being shot down because it did not apply to this case. This document shows the efforts of the JTFA and the results of their interviews with witnesses. The recommendations are sound and an underwater survey has not been done to date although the team recommended it. Only by searching the wreck for these remains can the family of Frank Bowman achieve closure. It is fairly certain that no evidence of his body washing up on shore exists therefore the bone fragments on the wreck of PCF-19 hold the only remains to be recovered of Frank Bowman, MIA since June 16th, 1968.)

On 4 February 1994, a letter updating the Young Family was received. The only new data is as follows:

On 5 October 1993, the Vietnamese Government repatriated the remains turned over to a joint team in August 1993. The remains are currently under analysis by forensic specialists. (Authors note: The remains were verified as those belonging to BM2 Anthony Chandler.)

On 3 March 1994, the Young Family from the Department of the Navy, Bureau of Naval Personnel, received a new letter with additional information.

On 17 January 1994, the American Contingent of the Joint U.S. /Vietnam Investigation Team arrived in Dong Ha, Town of Quang Tri Province to begin investigations of cases in this province during the 27th Joint Field Activity. The Team consisted of eight Americans including linguists, team medic and an explosive ordnance disposal technician. The Vietnamese on the team consisted of a representative of the Ministry of Foreign Affairs, two members of the Ministry of National Defense, two members of the Ministry of Interior, and five members of the Province People's Committee.

On the morning of 20 January 1994, the team traveled to Cua Tung Beach, (Grid Coordinates YD250827), Vinh Quang Village, Vinh Linh District to investigate case 1210. The first witness interviewed was Mr. Hoang Ngoc Dung, The People's Committee Chairman of Trung Giang Village, Gio Linh District. Mr. Dung provided testimony during the 25th JFA Investigation on this case. Mr. Dung informed the team that neither he, nor any other of the previous witnesses had any new information regarding this case.

The team next interviewed Mr. Bui Xuan Tu, a 27-year-old adult fisherman and resident of Hamlet 9, Trung Giang Village. He provided the following information:

1) In June or July of 1991, Mr. Tu was out diving for lobsters and fish approximately three kilometers off the coast of Hamlet 9, when he saw the wreckage of a boat approximately 14 meters underwater. Only the stern portion was above the ocean floor with the rest of the boat buried in sand and silt. Mr. Tu said the stern was four to five meters wide and estimated the overall length of the boat to be about 15 meters.

2) Mr. Tu returned to the site many times during the following months to salvage scrap metal from the wreck. He used explosives to clear the buried wreckage and get access to the metal. During these operations, Mr. Tu noticed many small, finger-sized bone fragments in the boat, which he did not retrieve.

3) According to Mr. Tu, other fishermen also dove on the wreckage and used explosives to recover scrap metal. He specifically cited Mr. Toan and Mr. Tao, who hired divers from Ha Tinh Province and recovered the boat's propeller. To Mr. Tu's knowledge, the only remains ever recovered from the wreck was a portion of thighbone recovered by Mr. Thu.

4) Mr. Tu claimed there is still wreckage at the site, but believes it would be difficult to find remains there now, due to all of the explosives used to salvage metal and the subsequent drifting of sand and silt over the wreckage.

The last witness interviewed was Bui Xuan Toan, a 26-year-old adult fisherman and resident of Hamlet 9, Trung Giang Village. Mr. Toan is the younger brother of Mr. Bui Xuan Tao, who was interviewed during the 25th JFA Investigation of this case. Mr. Toan provided the following information:

1) In approximately May of 1991, Mr. Toan and his brother, along with two divers from Ha Tinh Province (Mr. Ngu and Mr. Nhoe) salvaged metal from the wreckage of a boat approximately three kilometers offshore. Mr. Toan himself dove with the two divers while his brother stayed in a boat on the surface to run the air pumps for the divers.

2) The boat lies about 14 meters underwater with only the stern section visible. The stern was about three to four meters wide and Mr. Toan did not see any markings on the boat. Mr. Toan saw many small bone fragments inside the wreckage and claims the Mr. Ngu recovered one dogtag which he kept. Mr. Toan does not know the name that was on the dogtag. The divers used explosives to salvage metal from the wreckage, which is mostly covered with silt.

3) Mr. Toan showed the team a rusted barrel of an M-16 rifle, which he claims to have salvaged from the wreckage. There were no serial numbers or other markings on the barrel.

4) Material Evidence: None.

5) Survey Results: N/A.

6) Recommended future actions: Recommend this case be placed in the pending category.

7) Pertinent location or data changes: None.

8) Areas or case file information not investigated: None.

9) Analyst Comments:

   A. Prior to the investigation of this case, the VNOSMP attempted to locate the two divers in Ha Tinh Province who may be in possession of an identification tag and further information regarding disposition of remains. They reported that there is no Thang Loi Hamlet, in Ky Anh District of Nghe An Province. However, there are two village cooperatives named

Thang Loi. There was a Mr. Ngu at one of these cooperatives but no one is sure if this is the same Mr. Ngu found in Ref B. Allegedly the Mr. Ngu from this cooperative has moved to Minh Hai Province.

B. None of the witnesses provided any new information regarding the location or disposition of the wreckage.

10) Search and Recovery Specialist Comments: N/A.
11) Team Chief Comments:

A. During this 27th JFA, the Team received excellent support from the Vietnamese Government. This includes both Central Government and province contingents.
B. All locations found in this report were obtained using the global positioning system (GPS) with an accuracy of at least three satellite vectors.
C. The Team interviewed five witnesses who appeared to present their information in a straightforward and unrehearsed manner. The Team felt no attempt on the part of the witnesses to intentionally mislead them.
D. There are no remaining known witnesses with information concerning this case. Recommend this case be placed in the pending category.

(Authors note: There you have it, word for word from the report. No new witnesses and no new information reported. Therefore, the case will be placed in the pending category. Here are the questions still to be answered before the case is closed:

1) Why was there no attempt to dive on the wreckage to determine the exact location and the condition of the wreck?
2) With all the technology available to the U.S. Military as well as available from the Vietnamese Government, why is there not an attempt to salvage the bone fragments since this is the only evidence of remains possible for QM2 Frank Bowman?
3) It appears that it was more important to locate the dog tag than it was to locate the wreckage of PCF-19.
4) What has happened since 1994 to this case? A recommendation was made after the first investigation in 1993 to do a feasibility assessment for underwater recovery of this site. Once the remains were identified as belonging to BM2 Anthony Chandler, there has been no further attempt to locate remains of QM2 Frank Bowman. Surely, the many bone fragments described by witnesses on the wreck have a real possibility of belonging to Frank Bowman since he was in the forward cabin with the other two men killed, EN2 Ed Cruz and GMG2 Billy Armstrong.
5) Why was there never an investigation to explain what happened to the body of Anthony Chandler since HM1 Larry Lail insists he processed paperwork and delivered three bodies to the IUWG launch at 2300 on June 17th. Why did it take

two more days for these men to be processed by "C" Med and deliver them to the mortuary? Many Marines including two Australian Sailors delivered earlier that day were processed as well as many Marines on June 18th and 19th, before Armstrong and Cruz showed up on the mortuary logs.

6) Why is the same attention to resolving this case not assigned to resolving what could be an easy MIA resolution?

These and many other questions plague this author as he reviewed the evidence over the years. Only time will tell us if these issues are or can be resolved in the near future

CHAPTER SIXTEEN

Some Final Answers

On July 20, 1968, a message from CINCPAC to SECDEF and others gave the results of the informal Board of Investigation convened in Danang. Here are some of the findings of that board.

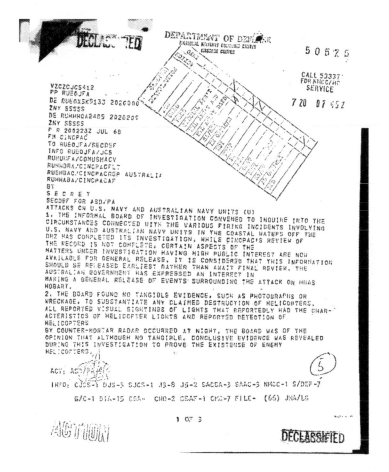

Figure 57. Message Traffic Detailing Results of Informal Board of Inquiry Page One.

The Board found no tangible evidence, such as photographs or wreckage, to substantiate any claimed destruction of helicopters. All reported visual sightings of lights that reportedly had the characteristics of helicopter lights and reported detection of helicopters by counter-mortar radar occurred at night. The Board was of the opinion that although

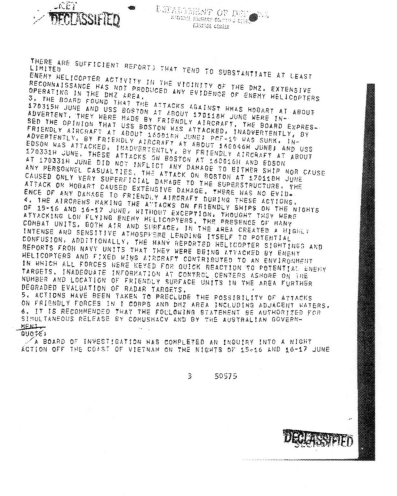

Figure 58. Message Traffic, Informal Board of Inquiry Page Two.

no tangible, conclusive evidence was revealed during this investigation to prove the existence of enemy helicopters, there are sufficient reports that tend to substantiate at least limited enemy helicopter activity in the vicinity of the DMZ. Extensive reconnaissance has not produced any evidence of enemy helicopters operating in the DMZ area. (Authors note: Apparently, the eye witness testimony of the Marines and sailors offshore as well as Swift Boat and Coast Guard Sailors didn't count for anything. Although no daylight sightings or wreckage occurred of these helicopters, the radar was considered unreliable as well.)

The Board found that although the attacks against HMAS Hobart at about 170315H June and USS Boston at about 170116H June were inadvertent, they were made by friendly aircraft. The Board expressed the opinion that USS Boston was attacked, inadvertently, by friendly aircraft at about 160010H June, and USS Edson was attacked, inadvertently, by friendly aircraft at about 170331H June. These attacks on Boston at 160010H and Edson at 170331H June did not inflict any damage to either ship or cause any personnel casualties. The attack on Boston at 170116H June caused only very superficial damage to the superstructure. The attack on Hobart caused extensive damage; there was no evidence of any damage to friendly aircraft during these actions.

The aircrews making the attacks on friendly ships on the nights of 15-16 and 16-17 June, without exception, thought they were attacking low flying enemy helicopters. (Authors note: Earlier in this message it is reported that there were no evidence of enemy helicopters operating in the DMZ area.

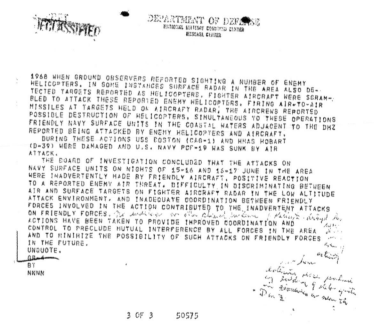

Figure 59. Message Traffic, Informal Board of Inquiry Pg. Three.

What then were the friendly aircraft sent up north to attack?) The presence of many combat units, both air and surface, in the area created a highly intense and sensitive atmosphere lending itself to potential confusion. Additionally, the many reported helicopter sightings and reports from Navy units that they were being attacked by enemy helicopters and fixed wing aircraft contributed to an environment in which all forces were keyed for quick reaction to potential enemy targets. Inadequate information at control centers ashore on the number and location of friendly surface units in the area further degraded evaluation of radar targets. (Authors note: This explanation is correct for the attacks on Boston and Hobart during the night hours of June 16-17. However, this was not the case on the previous night when PCF-19 was attacked and sunk. The weapons were different, the scenario was different, and PCF-19 was a much smaller target than Boston or Hobart. It is important to understand that this part of the message does not distinguish between the two nights when it explains the environment in which the attacking American jets found themselves. On the previous night June 15-16, they were hunting helicopter type targets reported by the Marines traveling between the mainland and Tiger Island. The next night the American jets were hunting the same targets but were aware by this time that an American Patrol Boat had been sunk and there were numerous Naval Units offshore in the immediate area. These Naval Units had radar and communications with which to direct the aircraft to the targets they were seeking. Could they all have been asleep at their consoles? I think not.)

Actions have been taken to preclude the possibility of attacks on friendly forces in I Corps and DMZ area including adjacent waters. The following statement was released by COMUSMACV and the Australian Government. Quote:

A board of investigation has completed an inquiry into a night action off the coast of Vietnam on the nights of 15-16 and 16-17 June 1968 when ground observers reported sighting a number of enemy helicopters. In some instances radar in the area also detected targets reported as helicopters. Fighter aircraft were scrambled to attack these reported enemy helicopters, firing air-to-air missiles at targets held on aircraft radar. The aircrews reported possible destruction of helicopters. Simultaneous to these operations, friendly Navy surface units in the coastal waters adjacent to the DMZ reported being attacked by enemy helicopters and aircraft.

During these actions, USS Boston (CAG-1) and HMAS Hobart (D-39) were damaged and U.S. Navy PCF-19 was sunk by air attack. (Authors note: Herein lies the problem with this theory. The above report describes the activity that resulted in the attacks on Boston and Hobart, and then adds PCF-19 was sunk by air attack. It does not differentiate the difference between the two nights and the different conditions that existed on these two nights, By doing so, it makes the public believe that both were attacked on the same night and by the same aircraft. It is important to remember that these are two significant events and even the weapons used were different, air to air missiles hit Hobart and Boston, and air to surface rockets hit PCF-19.)

The Board of Investigation concluded that the attacks on Navy Surface Units on nights of 15-16 and 16-17 June in the area were inadvertently made by friendly aircraft, positive reaction to a reported enemy air threat, difficulty in discriminating between air and surface targets on fighter aircraft radar in the low altitude attack environment, and inadequate coordination between friendly forces involved in the action contributed to the inadvertent attacks on friendly forces. Actions have been taken to provide improved coordination and control to preclude mutual interference by all forces in the area and to minimize the possibility of such attacks on friendly forces in the future. UNQUOTE.

It should be noted here that the same statements were made about providing improved coordination and control after two U.S. Air Force jets shot up USCG Point Welcome in 1966 off the DMZ despite repeated attempts to communicate with the aircraft. One of the results of this earlier attack was to paint a large white star on a blue circle on the pilothouse or cabin of all Naval Small Patrol Craft including the Coast Guard Vessels. Nothing was learned in the two years that passed between these two incidents. Rear Admiral Roy F. Hoffmann, USN, Retired, who was Captain Hoffmann, Commander Coastal Task Force 115 (Market Time) call sign "Latch", at this time would relate to me in 2004, the contents of a meeting held in Saigon after the incident with the top Commanders of the Allied Services with General Abrams. During this meeting, each of them was asked for suggestions on how to control the aircraft proceeding to and from targets over land and sea. He said they still could not agree on giving up tactical control of their aircraft to another branch of the service. Intra service rivalry is a complicated issue especially during wartime.

During the writing of this book, I talked to a former "Wild Weasel" pilot about the weapons aboard F-4 Phantoms. He suggested that I post a note on the website of the 366th TFW looking for information. Here is a reply from a Ronnie Houston; he gave me permission to use his statement. Quote:

I was a Weapons System Officer in F-4's from May 1969 through March 1974. During that time I flew in and am very familiar with the F-4C, F-4D, and F-4E. During 1969, all three models were stationed in SEA. The E's were in Korat, Thailand, the C's were at Cam Ranh Bay, and the D's were at Danang, Phu Cat, Ubon and Udorn. The Navy flew B's and J's, neither of which carried an internal gun.

I was stationed at Phu Cat during almost the entire year of 1970 where we flew only D Models. The only model that had a machine gun built into the aircraft was the E. Both the C and D models could however, carry a Suu16 machine gun on an external pylon. As a matter of course, that did not happen very often. As a matter of fact, the 366th TFW at Danang was nicknamed "Gunfighters" because they were the first to hang an external gun, around 1965 or '66.

AIM 9's and AIM 4's are missiles, not unguided rockets. They are primarily effective against an airborne target by their very nature. The AIM 9 Sidewinder is heat seeking and could conceivably be fired at a boat, however this certainly is outside the normal use and most likely would be unsuccessful. The same can be said for the AIM 4 Sparrow, except it is radar guided.

This type of gun (Suu16) was also used by helicopter gunships, Spooky, as well as C130's. It was very effective against troops and trucks. Oh yes, helicopters did have it, only in a smaller caliber. I believe it was 7.62 mm.

No Model of the F-4 can hover. Never could, never will.

Ronnie Houston
Woodlands, Texas "Unquote"

(Authors Note: I feel that this sums up the argument that an F-4 could not have hit the PCF-19 with any weapon she had nor were there such weapons as shot at Point Dume and PCF-12 aboard an F-4 Phantom.)

The Great Helicopter Mystery

The news that South Vietnamese officials flashed from I Corps last week was nothing less than astonishing: swarms of North Vietnamese helicopters had been sighted in the Demilitarized Zone, they claimed, and more than a dozen had been brought down by allied fire. Thus began the Great Helicopter Mystery.

Beginning two weeks ago and lasting for several nights, allied counter-mortar radar along the eastern edge of the DMZ, where the zone is bordered by the South China Sea, had indeed showed blips that looked like slow-moving, low-flying aircraft—like helicopters. American artillerymen had also reported sighting a series of strange moving lights near the Ben Hai River, the dividing line between North and South Viet Nam. Artillery and aircraft promptly opened fire on the targets and the blips disappeared.

No visual sightings of helicopters were made, and reconnaissance planes found no wreckage. But at about the same time as the U.S. response, several strange things happened. A U.S. Navy patrol boat was sunk off the DMZ by unidentified fire, the nearby Australian destroyer H.M.S. Hobart was holed in at least 200 places by what turned out to be three U.S. air-to-air Sparrow missiles, and three other vessels, including the cruiser U.S.S. Boston, reported that they had been fired on.

Opinion as to what had happened seesawed. Some officers thought it "highly probable" that a misreading of radar signals—images that looked like slow-moving helicopters but were really friendly vessels patrolling offshore—caused the allies to fire on their own ships. At week's end, while a special board of inquiry tried to fathom the mystery, U.S. officials in Saigon allowed that North Vietnamese helicopters might indeed have been in action in the DMZ. Whether or not they have come that far south, big Russian-built helicopters are now a standard part of North Viet Nam's much-improved weaponry.

24

Brothers Meet While In Navy

Thomas W. Fritz, FTG3, serving aboard the destroyer, USS Hanson, on duty off the Vietnam coast, recently met his brother, Lt. jg. Ronald E. Fritz during a stop-over in Japan.

Lt. Fritz, on temporary assignment in Japan, while his ship, the Point Dume, U.S.C.G.C., is in repair, has been joined there by his wife. Mrs. Fritz plans to remain in Japan until sometime in May, after which Lt. Fritz will return to Vietnam.

They are sons of Mr. and Mrs. Francis P. Fritz, 22 Quintal Drive, Westminster.

radar screens showed blips moving low and slowly, as invading helicopters might if hugging the waves for concealment. Once aloft, the Phantoms soon had moving blips on their own radar screens and unleashed Sparrow rockets at the targets. An eager South Vietnamese officer reported that 13 Communist helicopters had been destroyed.

On the same nights, a number of allied ships reported being attacked by enemy aircraft. That, too, had never happened in the war. Seven miles offshore near the DMZ, three shells narrowly missed the U.S.S. Boston. A 50-ft. patrol boat was sunk, taking five of her U.S. crew down with her. The Australian destroyer H.M.A.S. Hobart was hit by three rockets that killed two of her sailors.

Last week a U.S. board of investigation confirmed the tragic error that had been suspected ever since two survivors of the patrol boat had said that they had been attacked by a U.S. plane and the fragments of rockets that hit the Hobart had turned out to be Sparrow parts. What the spotters and pilots had taken for helicopters on their radar was, said the board, the allied ships. The pilots, of course, never saw their actual targets. The Sparrows are guided by radar and computers.

A covey of North Vietnamese helicopters might have triggered the whole chain of disastrous events and escaped before the Phantoms were airborne. But the board said that no evidence has been produced of enemy helicopter action near the DMZ. For the future, the U.S. command in Saigon promised that "action has been taken to provide improved coordination and control" of allied forces to prevent any repetition of June's deadly miscalculations.

VIET NAM WAR
Fatal Error   TIME, AUGUST 9, 1968

On two successive nights last June, U.S. F-4 Phantom jets scrambled to intercept what they took to be North Vietnamese helicopters, spotted for the first time crossing the Demilitarized Zone between North and South Viet Nam. The sightings were made by U.S. counter-mortar radar teams atop the hills overlooking the South China Sea. Their

Figure 60. Follow up Newspaper Clippings

The above clippings reflect the follow-up story in the media after this announcement of the findings of the Board of Inquiry. The results of the Formal Board of Inquiry held at CINCPAC in Hawaii, which concluded in September or October are buried in the archives of the Defense Department and I have been unable to locate them. The findings of both inquiries were the same, friendly fire on both nights. It is interesting to note that the Vietnamese accounts in 1993 and 1994 do not mention helicopters at all, they use witnesses from a village, believed to be abandoned at that time and state that the attacks came from shore based artillery. They do not report seeing any of the aircraft that responded to the incident nor the rescue and recovery operation that took place right offshore in the days following the attack on PCF-19. They do not mention the day and night bombing and shelling of the area by aircraft and Naval Units following these attacks as well.

The USCG Point Dume, Commanded by Ltjg Ron E. Fritz, would be awarded the Meritorious Unit Commendation for heroic achievement by the Secretary of the Navy. This took place on May 23rd, 1969 and was awarded to the Coast Guard WPB for rescuing the survivors of PCF-19 and after transporting them to medical facilities in Cua Viet, returned to the scene to search for possible survivors. Point Dume, along with PCF-12, received heavy automatic weapons fire from unidentified aircraft on two occasions. By maneuvering at high speed and by returning fire, the cutter was successful in suppressing fire from these aircraft without sustaining personnel casualties or material damage. Point Dume was awarded the Combat Action Ribbon for actions on June 16th, 1968 as well as other engagements. To be awarded the Combat Action Ribbon, personnel and or watercraft must be fired on by hostile forces and return fire.

In a Stars and Stripes article dated Monday August 26th, 1968, a North Vietnamese prisoner seized by American troops in a sweep of the small village of Dong Bao, Vietnam said he had been flown by helicopter to enter South Vietnam. He told South Vietnamese newsmen and field police that about one month ago his unit left Hanoi and went to Ninh Binh, where he and 15 other soldiers boarded a large, single rotor helicopter. They made

16 miles southeast of Da ....
Three U.S. Navy Swift boats and a Vietnamese Navy gunboat repulsed the attack.
. A Navy landing craft was sunk Thursday by an underwater explosion on the Cua Viet River 70 miles northwest of Da Nang. Six crewmen received minor injuries.

over the same target Thursday.
Lt. Carter B. Refo, who flew one of the attacks Friday, said, "I counted six different fires burning from our first run, and we got six more from our other runs. I hit a gasoline storage tank and a fireball leaped into the air in a high rolling column.

Irregular Defense ~ troops whose camp nea.. Lap in Quang Duc Province b.. been surrounded.

Thursday evening the bombers flew five missions, hitting troop concentrations, base camps and infiltration routes.

L e i. could b. time.

In the c: of living in to 112 wh Army serg: with a wil will draw ! stead of $2 tain (83) wi of depende $2.25 daily

Says Copters Ferry N. Viet Troops

DONG BAO, Vietnam (AP)— A North Vietnamese prisoner seized by American troops in a sweep of this small village Wednesday said he was flown by helicopter to enter South Vietnam.
The 25-year-old prisoner, who said he was a private, told South Vietnamese newsmen and field police that about one month ago

his unit left Hanoi and went to Ninh Binh, about 55 miles south of Hanoi, where he and 15 other soldiers boarded a large, single-rotor helicopter.
They made a four-hour flight, he said, and landed in a small jungle clearing. From there, they made a four-hour march to a camp in South Vietnam to prepare for attacks against allied troops, he said.
North Vietnam is known to have Russian-made medium and

heavy helicopters.
If what the prisoner said is true, it is most probable that his unit was flown about 300 miles south, which would have p'aced the helicopter landing zone a few miles north of the Demilitarized Zone.
A four-hour night march with local guides along infiltration routes could have taken the North Vietnamese soldiers through the six-mile wide buffer zone.

ROKs Ki

SAIGON forces kille light skirm: covered a camp, vict terrorist at operations.

🔺 **Pacific Stars & Stripes**
Monday, August 26, 1968

Figure 61. Stars and Stripes Clipping of August 26th, 1968.

a four-hour long flight, he said, and landed in a small jungle clearing. From there, they made a four-hour march to a camp in South Vietnam to prepare for attacks against Allied troops, he said. North Vietnam is known to have Russian-made medium and heavy helicopters. If what the prisoner said is true, it is most probable that his unit was flown about 300 miles south, which would place the helicopter-landing zone a few miles north of the Demilitarized Zone. A four-hour night march with local guides along infiltration routes could have taken the North Vietnamese soldiers through the six-mile wide buffer zone.

(Authors note: This report dated late in August, two months after the PCF-19 was sunk did not receive nationwide coverage in the U.S. Media even though reports of sightings of these lighted helicopter type aircraft continued throughout July and August by Allied troops and Naval patrol craft.)

One of the tragedies of this story is that during our search for witnesses, we were finally able to locate John Anderegg only to find that he had died in a car crash in Danville, Illinois. He was married to Connie Jean Silvey in 1972 and is survived by three daughters. His widow, now Mrs. Connie Messenger, remarried and lives in Fithian, Illinois. She provided several items of information about her late husband including a citation for a Silver Star, awarded to him for Conspicuous Gallantry during the rescue of his skipper, Ltjg John Davis and his attempts to save the life of his crewmate, QM2 Frank Bowman, who had escaped the PCF-19 before it sank. Badly wounded and unable to hold on to the also badly wounded Frank Bowman, his crewmate died in his arms and slipped beneath the surface of the South China Sea. His body was never recovered and he is still listed as MIA.

THE UNITED STATES OF AMERICA
THIS IS TO CERTIFY THAT
THE PRESIDENT OF THE UNITED STATES OF AMERICA
HAS AWARDED THE

SILVER STAR MEDAL

TO
JOHN R. ANDEREGG
GUNNER'S MATE SEAMAN, USN
FOR
GALLANTRY IN ACTION

IN SOUTHEAST ASIA ON 16 JUNE 1968

Figure 62. Silver Star Awarded to Anderegg.

The above copy of the certificate is not very good but shows that a Silver Star was indeed awarded to GMGSN John Anderegg for his actions on June 16th, 1968. After recovering from his wounds, John would return to active duty and was discharged at the end of his enlistment. John Davis tried many times to contact his crewman in the years after his recovery but was unable to find him. He was unable to get the Navy to assist him in finding Anderegg or did not know whom to contact.

DEPARTMENT OF THE NAVY
BUREAU OF NAVAL PERSONNEL
WASHINGTON, D.C. 20370

IN REPLY REFER T:
Pers-G25-MB/,
Oct 18, 1968

From: Chief of Naval Personnel
To: Commanding Officer
      Naval Hospital
      Great Lakes, Illinois 60088

Award in the case of GMSN John R. ANDEREGG, USN, B51 99 83; transmittal of

(a) SECNAVINST 1650.1C, Art. 224

(1) Silver Star Medal
(2) Citation and Certificate

1. The Chief of Naval Personnel takes pleasure in forwarding with congratulations, enclosure (1) and accompanying citation and certificate, enclosure (2), awarded to subject person.

2. It is requested that the presentation of this award be made in accordance with the provisions of reference (a). Please advise the Chief of Naval Personnel (Attn: Pers-G25) when the presentation has been accomplished.

M. H. Barns
M. H. BARNS
By direction

Figure 63. Endorsement Letter for Silver Star for Anderegg.

The Silver Star Award is dated October 18th, 1968, which is after the Board of Inquiry determined it was "friendly fire". Silver Star's are not awarded for non-hostile fire actions although a Purple Heart can be awarded for injuries sustained by "friendly fire" during an engagement with hostile forces. John Anderegg was a very brave young man that night and the Navy recognized his bravery by awarding this medal to him.

On June 16th, 2001, at a small cemetery in Warner Robbins, Georgia, the remains of BM2 Anthony Chandler were laid to rest. The family consisting of his mother Bessie Young, his step father Jack Young, his sister Jan Tadeo, and his brother Joe Young, surrounded by a rifle squad, many Swift Boat Sailors, other family and friends watched as his casket was placed above his final resting place. In an article by Mr. Travis Fain, a reporter for the Macon Telegraph dated June 17th, 2001, he would reflect: A group of bikers stood off away from the service, quiet in leather vests and jackets. None of them ever met Tony Chandler, they said, but still they knew him well. "He's our brother," said Stanley Amey, a Vietnam Veteran living in Bonaire. "We came to welcome him home."

Others there included several officers from the Swift Boat Sailors Assn, an organization of Swift Boat Veterans founded in 1995. Pete Sullivan, the NGLO ashore that night came from New Hampshire to pay his respects. Larry Lail, the corpsman who insists that he processed the body of Chandler on the deck of USS Acme along with three others of the crew was there to say good-bye. This author was there as well, coming from California to watch a fellow Swiftie and a part of this story carried so long in his head laid to rest. Arnold Feller, one of the divers that recovered the remains of the crew on June 16th and 17th, 1968 drove all night from his home in Florida to be there and to give his condolences to the family. It was a very hot day in Warner Robbins as this group of about 100 people observed this somber ceremony. One member of the honor guard collapsed from the heat but after a drink of water rejoined the group standing in honor. Jan Tadao, Tony's sister would reflect that her mother, Bessie had taken the "not knowing part" very hard and now she seems to be at peace. Now her mother has "a place to put flowers on from time to time", she said. His brother Joe Young always felt that he died for nothing especially after the "friendly fire" decision. He and Jan were 10 and 12 years old when the terrible news was brought home that their brother would not be coming home. Joe felt like he was just on a 50 foot boat, how was that important? (To the war) Why did he have to die? His anger and bitterness have lessened over the years. Swift Boat Sailors he was told served a crucial role and saved many lives. "It kind of eases the pain," Joe said. "Maybe his sacrifice saves other American Boys lives." A POW/MIA flag accompanied the Color Guard out of rememberance for those still listed as missing in Southeast Asia. Swifties consider these dead and missing brothers as "still on patrol" and will never be forgotten.

Larry Lail expressed his hope that remains of Frank Bowman can indeed be found and recovered from the wreck of PCF-19 even after all these years. We believe they are there,

BM2 Anthony G. Chandler
October 21, 1944   June 16, 1968

Figure 64. BM2 Anthony Chandler is from Warner Robbins, GA

the Vietnamese Fisherman reported them there and all that is needed is to recover them and bring the same closure to the Bowman family.

Figure 65.GMG2 Billy Armstrong is from West Helena, Arkansas.

Figure 66. EN2 Edward Cruz is from Inarajan, Guam.

There are no pictures of Mui Quang Thi, the South Vietnamese Interpreter aboard this crew but he is remembered as well. A small but early picture of QM2 Frank Bowman is all we have found of him in uniform. He remains missing in action and is remembered as one man his fellow Swifties do not want to leave behind.

Figure 67. QM2 Frank Bowman is from Walterboro, South Carolina.

(Authors Note: The pictures of the PCF-19 Crew shown here are courtesy of Joe Muharsky, a Swiftie who has a website showing pictures of all the Swiftie KIA's. Thank you Joe.)

Swift Boat Sailors everywhere would like to see him buried in our lifetime. Forty-nine Swifties lost their lives in Vietnam aboard these small but able gunboats both offshore and in the rivers and canals of the Mekong Delta. They will not be forgotten.

CHAPTER SEVENTEEN

Epilogue

In this book, I have tried to separate myth from fact, truth from fiction. I used copies of official documents once classified and now released under the "Freedom of Information Act". It has taken ten years to locate, document and research the information in this book. I found men who carried parts of this incident in their heads all these years, as did I. I was determined to write this story regardless of the fact that the Official Findings will never be changed. In the political climate of 1968 with America's thoughts of war and ending it on most of their minds it was easy to bring a quick closure to this incident by calling it "friendly fire" and moving on. The media was satisfied and a war weary public felt that it was "just one of those accidents in war". I took the facts as I know them, coupled with testimony from other Marine, Navy, Coast Guard, and Air Force Veterans who were there and told the story as all of us believe it really happened. I make the argument that given the proper atmosphere and time to investigate all areas of this incident a different finding may have been reached. I believe that this book will inform and comfort the many people involved by bringing information previously unknown to them. It will also bring attention to the men and women of the Joint Task Force for POW/MIA's who labor tirelessly in jungle heat and cold climates to recover the remains of our comrades long held Missing in Action. The efforts of them to recover the remains of Anthony Chandler will forever be remembered by my fellow Swifties. To Dick Hite, a Senior Analyst with the JTFA who took the time to update Doc Lail and I when the efforts to locate remains of the PCF-19 crewman fell to his group. Doc Lail in turn was able to update the Young family in a more personal way as we sorted through the rest of the evidence in this case. Without the Internet, many hours by my friends on the telephone, and of course DNA technology, none of this would be possible.

In this book the following issues were accomplished to the best of my ability.

1) To inform the readers of the mission of Swift Boats to better understand the conditions under which these men were lost.

2) Using deck logs and personal accounts, to separate the incident of PCF-19 and the attacks on HMAS Hobart and USS Boston. These were two distinct and separate events with no question that the attacks on Hobart and Boston were

made by U. S. Air Force jets firing Sparrow Missiles at suspected airborne targets. A tragic loss of life and injuries occurred on board Hobart and my heart goes out to those families in Australia as they read this account.

3) PCF-19 was attacked and sunk by unidentified aircraft on June 15/16th that we believe belonged to North Vietnam. They had the helos and were equipped with the type of weapon that hit and sunk PCF-19. A similar rocket was fired at and missed PCF-12. These aircraft had the ability to "hover" and move at slow speeds as well as maneuver up and down. They also carried some type of machine gun which when fired at PCF-12 and Point Dume was answered with deadly fire that caused them to break contact. One helo believed to be shot down by the forward gunner aboard PCF-12, GMGSN Tom Klemash.

4) There is a distinct difference in the log entries at the Danang Mortuary between HM1 Larry "Doc" Lail's delivery of three bodies to an IUWG launch in Danang Harbor and the actual log entries. BM2 Chandler is noticeably missing as well as the odd times and days of entries. We believe there was a mix-up in the handling of these bodies and BM2 Chandler was indeed recovered on June 17th, 1968 from the wreck of PCF-19. Divers removed a pistol that could have only come from his body.

5) The U.S. Air Force responded to calls for help from the Marines along the DMZ who reported numerous "lighted aircraft" moving to and from Tiger Island. During the initial response, by two F-4 Phantom jets from the "Gunfighter Squadron" based in Danang, PCF-19 was hit and sunk by two rockets. Two rocket hits that did not resemble the damage done by Sparrow air-to-air missiles or Sidewinder air to air missiles. The flight patterns and movements of these supersonic jets did not reflect the movements reported by the Marines ashore and the Naval and Coast Guard personnel offshore. Unfortunately, one or more of these pilots was blamed for hitting the ships and PCF-19 was wrongly included in this account.

6) Accounts by the Vietnamese fishermen in the 1990's who dove on the wreck report numerous finger sized bone fragments on the wreck. This is the best chance of recovering remains of QM2 Frank Bowman and should be given top priority for recovery. It would be an "easy" recovery to solve another MIA case. These fishermen also report no evidence of helo activity and state that "shore artillery" sunk the PCF-19 and they saw no recovery or rescue operations after the sinking. They also seemed to have missed all the bombardment of the DMZ area that went on for several days after PCF-19 was sunk. These fishermen claim to be members of the "Village Militia" in an area held by the North Vietnamese and scenes of nearly non-stop combat between the NVA and the Marines.

This ends the story, the real story of the Sinking of PCF-19.

The End